CW01306262

EMERGENT MUSIC AND VISUAL MUSIC: INSIDE STUDIES

Part One: The Book

Ronald A. Pellegrino

Electronic Arts Productions

Copyright © 2009 by Ronald A. Pellegrino

All rights reserved
Printed in the United States of America

For information about permission to reproduce selections from this book, write to:
Permissions, Electronic Arts Productions
2128 Burning Tree Lane, Denton, Texas 76209 USA

Pellegrino, Ronald A.
Emergent music and visual music: inside studies / Ronald A. Pellegrino
1. Pellegrino, Ronald A. 2. Music composition. 3. Music theory.
4. Emergent music. 5. Visual music. 6. Cyberspirits. 7. Pythagoras.
8. Aesthetics. 9. Laser animation. 10. Audio engineering.
11. Video. 12. Psychophysics. 13. Memory.

Published by:
Electronic Arts Productions
2128 Burning Tree Lane
Denton, Texas 76209 USA

FOR MY DAUGHTER LISA

Contents

Preface   vi

ONE
Compositional Practice

1. Emergent Music   3
2. Composition In The Electronic Arts   7
3. Principles For Learning To Compose With Sound And Light   11
4. Discovering, Cultivating, And Using Your Own Voice   14
5. Compositional Field Tests   19
6. Omnimedia On The Road   21

TWO
Compositional Theory

7. An Ode To Electronic Instruments In The Arts   26
8. Common Ground: Psychophysics   31
9. Patterns of Nature: Rhythms Of Life   35
10. Levels of Algorithmic Composition   42
11. Compositional Algorithms As Cyberspirit Attractors   44
12. Matrix Alignment   50
13. The Crevices of Audio Compression   58
14. Why Care About Sonification   62

THREE
Visual Music

15. Visual Music Flavors   69
16. Graphic Scores   72
17. Playing Free Of The Video Box   74
18. The Hewlett-Packard Session   79
19. Suggestions For Using The Visual Music Studies   81

viii   Emergent Music And Visual Music: Inside Studies

FOUR
Pythagoras & Pellegrino In Petaluma

    20. Pythagoras In Petaluma   87
    21. Laser Animations And Pythagorean Thought   90
    22. The Laser Animation System   93
    23. The Laser Images   95
    24. Animated Laser Visual Music Meditations   97

FIVE
DVD Volume 1

Set One:
    1. Winter Reflections   103
    2. The Unison   105
    3. Cynthia's Dream   109
    4. Soft Candy   111
    5. Liquid Light   113

Set Two:
    6. Windswept   116
    7. SR HP Flight 4   121
    8. Nina's Song   122
    9. SR HP Flight 5   123
    10. SR HP Flight 8   124
    11. Deb Fox Tour One   125
    12. Deb Fox Tour Two   127

SIX
DVD Volume 2

Set One:
    1. Elizabeth   131
    2. SR HP Flight 2   132
    3. SR HP Flight 6   133
    4. SR HP Flight 3   134
    5. SR HP Flight 1   135

Set Two:
    6. Bliss & Contact Dance   136
    7. UW Rockers   138
    8. SR HP Flight 7   139
    9. Beyond The Event Horizon   140
    10. Deb Fox Additional Video Files   141
    11. Musings Collection One   142

SEVEN

DVD Volume 3: Pythagoras & Pellegrino In Petaluma

Sample Suite   145
Study 1 - Kate   146
Study 2 - Lia   147
Study 3 - Ray   148
Study 4 - Yo-Yo   149

EIGHT

DVD Volume 4: Pythagoras & Pellegrino In Petaluma

Study   5 - Malie   153
Study   6 - Keb   154
Study   7 - WAG   155
Study   8 - Nella   156
Study   9 - Astor   157
Study 10 - Meg   158

Glossary   159

Acknowledgments   165

Index   171

Preface

Imagine the notion of music as a multifaceted crystal. Each of the virtually infinite number of facets represents one possibility of the immense range of qualities that music embodies and projects. The power of your attention—how you direct and focus your history, desires, and intelligence—creates the light that attracts a receptive facet, thereby moving the crystal to align that facet with your point of view so as to set in motion a creative loop. In the field generated by such a loop, it's impossible to tell whether the light is reflected off the facet (your light) or emerges on its own, through the facet from the depths of the crystal (music's light). It really doesn't make any difference which view is taken if the object of the exercise is a ticket to the realm of the sublime.

The key to starting the emergent music engine is to create or to discover an environment, an algorithm, or a system configured to promote self-organization. Such a creation or discovery will help you break free of your programs—all those long-term memories that push you aside and compete with each other to steer your course in all that you do. Breaking free of your programs is critical for generating conditions that reveal the potential for experiencing the greatest number of facets. A closely related way of considering the process is to imagine that you can magically shake loose all those facets, and then place yourself, the composer, as a seed crystal in their midst to discover what new forms of music will emerge from that creative exercise.

In these studies visual music is one facet of what emerges from a deeply considered notion of music. As such, visual music is a form of emergent music. The operating principles that give rise to emergent music work equally well in all the performance arts.

The complete package for *Emergent Music And Visual Music: Inside Studies* comes in four parts—Part One: The Book, Part Two: The DVDs, Part Three: The CDs, and Part Four: Leading Experimentalists of the late 20th/early 21st Centuries. This item, Part One: The Book, is designed to lay the theoretical and historical groundwork for Part Two: The DVDs and Part Three: The CDs. Also it is intended to serve a number of other purposes as listed below:

1. To clarify the notions of Emergent Music and Visual Music.

2. To generate a feeling for and insight into the experimental process that drives the evolution of the electronic arts of sound and light.

3. To serve as a basis for visual music studies for any interested parties including practicing artists and students, in or out of academia.

4. To provide background theoretical and historical information that fleshes out the context for the material on the DVDs, Volumes 1 - 4.

5. To function as a guide providing insight into the thought and technical processes represented by the sound and light material on the DVDs.

6. To be of value as a standalone monograph on the realtime approach to composition, an approach that both serves to further an individual's development and to reflect the current state of that development.

7. To articulate the principles of realtime composition, an aesthetic position that integrates composition and performance in the electronic arts of sound and light and that applies equally well to other performance media.

In most cases the presentation of the material in this book is relatively informal, as if I were having conversations with friends, colleagues, or other interested parties at a cafe, over lunch, when they were making a visit to my studios, when they approached me after one of my concerts, or via email. I prefer this conversational style to what I was obliged to use for my first two books. *An Electronic Studio Manual* (1969) was initially one-third of my doctoral dissertation project, so the delivery was formal for academic purposes. *The Electronic Arts of Sound and Light* (1983) was published by Van Nostrand Reinhold, a company that specializes in reference books and distributes globally, so it was also more formal in its presentation. This go-around I'm choosing a publishing vehicle that encourages freedom of expression and avoids the impediments of bureaucratic formalities.

The presentational form of the package is like a record of a combination of visits over the years to my studios and to my public presentations. The materials are collections based on my personal preferences, ways I prefer to hear, to see, and to explore. What's included has also been shaped by the somewhat limited nature of the recording systems, specifically the video and DVD recording systems.

The studies can be used to get a sense of the rhythm of exploration in the performance context. The studies can also be thought of as a guided tour through the sound and light possibilities of my particular visual music system configurations—hardware, software, and protocompositional designs. The conceptual aspect of the configurations should be viewed as electronic ragas—collections of melodies, rhythms, and tunings that I've honed over the years to make them available as realtime compositional material—material to be used in a fashion very similar to the traditional approach the North Indian musicians have to their ragas.

After my ragas are developed over time, often many years in the making, a performance process naturally comes into play. A particular performance process grows out of the nature of a particular raga. One of the protocompositional problems in working with the ragas is to discover their inherent voices in terms of tempo, inflections, rhythms, and micro and macro shapes. The final result of the process is an exercise in realtime composition, an exercise that relies on the principle of "tuning on-the-fly," that is, making adjustments to compositional variables according to the needs of the moment.

What struck me in the late 1960s, when I first came across the oscillographic images (Lissajous figures) of harmonious sound, was that here was a special case for beauty that appeals to theoretical scientists and at the same time is highly seductive to just about anyone who witnesses the marriage of sound and imagery. What scientists often consider beautiful is born of a special kind of internal logic in the connections between their theories and what their experiments in reality demonstrate. Since that discovery in the late 1960s I have worked to find connections between sound and sight that work aesthetically for both the ear and the eye. That collection of sound/light connections constitutes the common ground shared by the ear and the eye. This is an emerging area of psychophysics full of practical as well as aesthetic applications. The virtual reality researchers are busy cashing in on the practical applications while the Visual Music Studies on these DVDs represent some aesthetic and instructive applications.

No map exists for this research. That's the case because the eye and the ear, that is seeing and hearing, have evolved over the eons for different evolutionary purposes, and the research tools for exploring their common ground have only become generally available during the past forty years or so. Searching for the common ground of the ear and the eye is one of the electronic art games I've been playing for most of my life with no specific purpose in mind other than the pleasure it affords. An area of research I've found most fruitful is the exploration of the interaction of wavetrains with fundamental frequencies that are integer ratios; that exploration leads directly to my studies of the work of Pythagoras.

I've used the sort of material found on the DVDs in a variety of applications including discovering for myself and teaching others to hear and to see more deeply and with greater detail. In a nutshell, the process involves using vision to guide hearing and hearing to guide vision.

In the visual music studies the experienced eye will notice a few glitches passed along from the original analog video recordings (analog tape is notorious for dropout as it ages), as well as other types of anomalies that are characteristic of media translations and media transpositions. In my view, there's much to be learned from studying relatively uncut, raw versions of the realtime compositional process in much the same way one would experience it sitting next to me in my studios or at my performances. The individual studies are various combinations of the sort of raw as well as more developed material you would expect to find in a composer's notebook or an artist's sketchpad.

With the advent of the internet I thought I would never need to write another book. My website seemed to be the perfect vehicle for passing along my work—what could be better than a globally distributed multimedia ebook? Then in late 2008 I decided that this present sort of a package is a far superior vehicle for distributing this information because it doesn't have to contend with the current internet data throughput drag that many of us continue to experience. Plus, standalone and computer DVD players handle this data-intensive material with ease, and you can have a book in your hand in front of or away from the video pieces. Also, I personally find there's a significant improvement in the quality of my attention when I read essays written in a book compared to reading similar material on a computer screen; others tell of a similar quality improvement.

The book and the DVDs are based on my personal experiences in the electronic arts of sound and sound since the 1960s; the personal historical references are best viewed in that light. Everything included has been the subject of countless private studio tests with an assortment of invited guests. It has also been the subject of many hundreds of my public performance field tests such as concerts and other presentations. In a sense, a significant part of the book can be considered a log of where I've been, when I was there, and what was on my mind at the time. It represents one approach to the electronic arts of sound and light, not the only approach and not necessarily the best for everyone, but certainly the only one I thought worth pursuing.

This package has been ten years in the making. The first steps were taken in the late 1990s when I recorded the laser animations to video, and that was not done initially with this project in mind. For unknown reasons, at that time I felt compelled to commit my laser work to a storage medium; that was a change of heart after a lifetime of arguments to myself and others against recording my laser work. I was also working on a large number of writing projects for my website during the latter half of the decade of the 1990s and, as I said above, I was convinced I'd never get involved in writing another book. However, in mid-2008 when I woke up to the inevitable fact that the clock is ticking down, I decided to pass along some of my great old synthesizers around which I built studios since the late 1960s. In the process of selling those instruments on eBay, I discovered that there's a generation or two of artists around the world who find of great value what those instruments represent. Yes, they love the hardware, and they seem equally fascinated by what it has done and what it can do for thinking as well as art making. Email exchanges with artists from all over the world were sufficient motivation for me to tie up all its loose ends and complete this project. I pray it's of value to the field.

ONE

Compositional Practice

1
Emergent Music

Emergent music is based on one of the key evolutionary imperatives, the creative principle that, through the process of procreation, leads to the generation of occasional variations rather than always exact replications. In lieu of the mechanics of natural selection, the composer, the person responsible for emergent music and visual music must play the roles of decision maker and guide—deciding which forms that emerge from compositional algorithms or systems are sufficiently significant, and then judiciously guiding those algorithms or systems that best tend toward self-organization to generate the most desirable forms.

Engaging in the process of creating emergent music has value beyond the music itself. It's a method for breaking free of the chains of memories that represent the web of all your neural programs put into place long before the culture released you and before you decided that you wanted to be free of its chains. We are who we are because of our memories and all the associations connected to those memories. The trick for any artist wanting to sample what it means to be original is to break free of those memories and associations. Designing compositional algorithms or systems for creating emergent music is one path to that freedom.

The process requires working a fine floating line between functioning as a creative artist or being a slave to the syndrome linked to being a victim of comfort and security. In most cases relying on memory leads to the comfort and security of predictability because memory will lead you to do what's easiest, what's already been done in the past. Long-term memory forms through repetition, shock, or inspiration. It takes considerable effort to make new memories, and, beyond childhood, the older one gets, the more difficult it is to do so. Furthermore, cultural programming is so insistent and so effective today that even our youngsters are set in their ways earlier and earlier in life. We live in a global economy that's designed to get you to trade your life for some trinkets, bonbons, Madison Avenue dreams, and perpetuation, and for the most part, that economic mindset also rules the arts. As a counterweight to the aforesaid, any process that creates a sense of freedom, however fleeting, is worthy of consideration; exploring compositional algorithms for creating emergent music is a leading candidate in the creative arts.

Typically, in the initial stages, the output of compositional algorithms is difficult to predict. Thus the composer of emergent music is required intuitively to make aesthetic judgments about the expressive value of the initial output and whether, with sculpting, it has the potential to inspire the sort of depth and breadth of feeling that will move human beings. When working with emergent music it's not uncommon to get the sense that you don't really own it. But rather that it's just yours to pass along for others to consider. And that's why I refer to my work in this book and the DVDs as studies.

Everything you see and hear in *Emergent Music and Visual Music: Inside Studies* is based on the following principles for composing emergent music:

1. Compose systems (sets of internally related parts) designed to evolve over time. The parts of those systems could include artists of all inclinations, electronic instruments, electronic functions, energy systems, previously composed systems, or anything capable of relational interactions.

2. Set a system in motion multiple times with as many different internal and external triggers, feedback loops, and influences as can be imagined.

3. Experiment with different configurations of the same set of parts, compare the outputs, and develop a language for articulating, notating, and recording what works best.

4. When a system begins to generate what you sense as desirable (your personal aesthetic judgments), fine-tune the variables so as to emphasize what you deem most desirable.

5. If you want to function as a composer beyond the original design of the system you must make aesthetic judgments even with systems that are eventually expected to make their own decisions (either by internal logic, by way of external influences, or a combination of the two). Assume authorship and whatever that may bring.

6. Accept the system's output as final, or collect a number of viable outputs and then work to combine or sequence them by traditional or invented means.

7. There is considerable value in studying complexity theory, although it isn't necessary for practicing artists to be seduced by its minutiae and to be drawn into the vortex of complexity theory as it's viewed by mathematicians and computer scientists.

8. Contemplate the notion of interacting multidimensional matrices and the myriad ways they can generate scenarios for emergence. See Chapter 12 on Matrix Alignment.

9. Invent or discover exercises that draw you away from the everyday world. For example, just pretend for the sake of adding extra spice to your existence:

    a) that you are more of a mystic than a mathematician. (Mystics have been among us at least as long as mathematicians, and perhaps you can say that historically mathematics is an outgrowth of mysticism, so in pretending to tap into your mystical roots you might actually open a floodgate that will enrich your life.)

    b) that as a privileged life form you're occupying a choice place in the womb of creation.

    c) that you're endowed with the power to sense possibilities becoming realities all around you.

    d) that you can choose to direct your energies to support emerging realities that contribute to the prime evolutionary imperative of ever more refined, ever more powerful, ever more aware and intelligent (thus beautiful) forms.

Ephemeral Forms: Mother Musings Flight Patterns is a title for concerts I used many times during the mid to late 1970s with a group I organized called The Real* Electric Symphony. This was a group that only worked in the realtime composition mode, a subset of Emergent Music. It involves solo or group on-the-fly decision-making based on bringing the histories of the participants to the leading edge of the evolving moment with the object of integrating those histories so what was unanticipated but still worthy becomes realized in sound and light. Our performance art forms emerged from flights of fancy—collaborative musings. To create emergent forms of value we worked to enter a compositional mode of thought that went far beyond the "anything goes, la-di-da" world of typical improvisation. The personnel in the group ranged from 3 to 50 in number and included electronic and acoustic musicians of all stripes, dancers, filmmakers, video artists, light sculptors, laser animators, poets, theater folks, and others who chose to come along for the ride.

Success in realtime composition is based on faith in your ability to recognize significant forms as they emerge during your explorations, to discern whether they're worth developing, and to remember them for future reference and application when suitable occasions arise. What makes forms significant is that they embody or reflect authentic feelings or perspectives and that these feelings or perspectives communicate to, connect with, and grow out of the fundamental human drive to promote the evolution of the senses and the higher levels of consciousness. Therefore, repeating what someone else has already done is wasteful unless it's an exercise to gain insight into their character and lay the groundwork for a deeper connection to their work. Sensing what to avoid is just as important as sensing what to include. Best avoided as waste are structures that result from formulas or comfortable schools of thought as well as those that have been drained of their affective power by overexposure.

The realtime compositional process is a continuing exercise in applying the principles of creative freedom. Exercising creative freedom presupposes the discipline to develop an awareness of and an ability to apply principles of composition that are part of the valued heritage of the human race. Finding a source for those principles requires more effort than many are willing to expend and requires some good luck to boot. Access via the expected sources is very difficult because our educational systems, even in the arts, tend to be mostly mechanical and materialistic in the sense that the practitioners trade in matter purposely designed to prepare people to be economic cogs in the societal system as either consumers or perpetuators of the system (unfortunately most teachers at all levels).

The individual who wants to explore the principles of creative freedom must commit to discovering them wherever possible and gravitating toward those practitioners who hold them in high esteem. If fortune smiles, one can choose to learn from those who value the integration of principles along with the technical side of the business of the arts. Again, luck always helps.

As a graduate student at the University of Wisconsin in the 1960s I just happened to be there at the same time as two musical giants and good friends in the very much inspirational latter stages of their careers, Rudolf Kolisch and René Leibowitz. Kolisch was a violinist with a long history of organizing string quartets that presented premieres of leading 20th century composers, including Arnold Schoenberg, Alban Berg, Anton Webern, and Béla Bartók. Leibowitz, who studied with both Ravel and Webern, practiced music as a composer, conductor, and theorist and was the teacher of Pierre Boulez among others.

Both Kolisch and Leibowitz functioned as advocates of the new music of their day by performing, conducting, teaching, and writing about their deeply held musical passions. The graduate seminars that they team-taught at the University of Wisconsin zoomed in and out of the music in ways that examined every note for its relationships to its immediate surroundings as well as to the whole. They managed to make musical ideas palpable by giving them meaning and life in ways that those being initiated could comprehend. I still clearly remember a stunningly moving concert of music by composers of the Second Viennese School that they co-produced using members of The University of Wisconsin student orchestra, most of them absolutely new to the music and depending completely on Kolisch and Leibowitz for their guidance. The UW students were taken by their ears to the very core of the music and managed to recreate it with beauty and conviction.

In their joint approach, Kolisch and Leibowitz, in addition to leading those of us in their seminars through a microanalysis of every musical detail, always managed to highlight all levels of structural principles, just the sort of ideas that any composer could assimilate and use as points of departure in his own work. Their analytical and theoretical approach underscored metatheoretical principles such as the functional relationships of individual voices, parts, and sections; independence; pivoting on shared attributes; counterpoint; texture; the dramatic; the lyrical; repetition schemes; multiple modes of variation; contrast; voicing; and many others.

Of course, just because they were supremely adept at leading us through the analysis of form and structural detail, that doesn't mean that everyone left their seminars with the desire to exercise musical freedom with what they had experienced. Kolisch and Leibowitz didn't preach freedom; instead they were living examples of what could be achieved by practicing it. Their lives demonstrated that to embrace and develop the principles of creative freedom requires a willingness to learn by doing, to leave the safety of the ground and risk some potentially embarrassing crashes, especially when you're not always among friendly fellow explorers. The artistic and intellectual richness of their lives and their work clearly showed that the return on the risk is worth the effort.

The key to working in the realm of emergent art forms is to cultivate a life dedicated to exploring what is known about past art forms, to participating in the realization of present art forms, and to engage in creating scenarios for realizing future art forms. When experienced inspirational practitioners are not available, the heavy digging needs to be done on your own. The study of any field that inquires into the evolution of form is fair game and that's just as true of the biological sciences as it is of astronomy, chemistry, physics, and any other field that analyzes the influences that give rise to shape and form over time. Learning to recognize emergent forms of communicative value is exactly the same as learning a new language—the more you practice and use it, the better you'll be at it.

For more information see Chapter 11 on Compositional Algorithms as Cyberspirit Attractors.

2
Composition
In The Electronic Arts

The traditional approach to composing western music is to make or create sound structures that unfold and evolve over time using material, elements, or parts that have been conceived, developed, and passed along through the history of the medium. Using that approach all you have to do to make a mark in the field is to make a little wiggle here or there, do it with some style and flair, and repeat it often enough so you can be identified. Nice work if you want it, and clearly many do.

The history of western music composition can be viewed from multiple perspectives, and finding one that feels right should be the first order of business for a budding composer. Nevertheless, it's rare for the issue of perspective to surface at all, early or late, because the structure of composition pedagogy is taken for granted by the vast majority of educational institutions—students take music theory classes (which are actually very limited studies in the history of music materials—sounds, structures, and instruments) and apply those lessons to solving composition problems usually of someone else's devising. Rarely encouraged are explorations of problems related to steering your own course, problems that involve psychology and philosophy that are both generalized and related to you in particular. If your teachers haven't been taught to steer their own course, how can they help you steer yours? Instead you're taught what they were taught—the traditional approach to composing western music (mostly mechanics—easier to grade, so a better fit for the institutional mindset). Unless you're very fortunate to find an environment that values and encourages the evolution of your particular brand of authenticity, you have to find your way on your own if you want to break out of that standard bubble, and that may require leaping into the abyss—scary but worth the risk.

Each global locale has its own history of its own music, and that history usually includes borrowed materials from other musical cultures either indigenous or from afar. Generations are glued together by the music of their time and generally view their music as a crucial separator from other generations. Subcultures, even in the same generation, define themselves through their music; and functional settings play an important role in that definition. The histories of various institutional musics run concurrently—commercial music, club music, church music, academic music, etc. What adds to the complexity of the music scene is that the nature of the institutions as well as the music change over time. Added to the relatively shorter time scales of generations, it's necessary to factor in the far longer time arches. For example, one way of viewing what we know of the past 700 years or so of western music is to consider it as a development from the simplest to the most complex relationships in the harmonic series, starting with the lowest number integer relationships and gradually continuing through and accumulating the higher number relationships.

What distinguishes composing in the electronic arts from composing with traditional media (such as the instruments of the orchestra) is that before you can compose in the electronic arts, you need either to discover or to create the material. Yes, someone can do that work for you and provide you with a basket of presets, but then the music of everyone who uses that basket tends to sound, look, and act the same. Listening to concerts based on such an approach to composition is like listening to a series of variations on a theme—not really such a bad idea for a student exercise, but not of much value for mature composers expected to make contributions to the culture. Clearly in concerts of music based on such an approach, a composer's authenticity has little value. Outside of the electronic arts a perfect example of that approach to composition that found a home in the academic world during the mid-20th century was the serial movement. The music was the result of all head and no heart, and many a concert goer suffered plenty of pain in their conscientious attempts to find even an iota of redeeming grace in the endless variations of those twelve-tone rows.

It's true that in the 20th century we were graced with rare birds such as Harry Partch and Salvatore Martirano and a few other composers, who built their own instruments and designed their own musical strategies from scratch. They made unmistakably original (authentic) music with those instruments and strategies, but they were...rare birds. When it appeared on the scene in the 1960s the concept of an electronic music synthesizer was a major breakthrough because it made the way of thinking about music exemplified by Partch and Martirano more generally available. The invitation that synthesizers extend to composers is to become an instrument designer or what's more commonly called today, a sound designer. That newfound freedom can extend to sound environments which can be collections of newly invented instruments—a new orchestra by another name. That's a special twist in the evolutionary spiral because a greater number of composers, if they so choose, can become involved in the movement that celebrates the realization of their individual gifts. They don't have to conform to the old standard approach. Instead, if we're fortunate, the gathering critical mass will probably lead to a truly open standard approach which embraces authenticity, and that will greatly benefit new composers, most likely without either their knowledge or appreciation of the history of the various approaches that led to the newfound freedom.

The best material for sound design is only discovered through an exploratory process. That process is facilitated by releasing preconceptions and being open to the unexpected; that's much easier said than done because traditional educational systems have subjected most young composers to intense programming focused on building techniques and studying the history of techniques. Nevertheless, even in the early 21st century, more than four decades after synthesizers emerged and despite, from the earliest days, almost constant pressure from academics to standardize the field, it's still possible to achieve a free state of being in the electronic arts. However the freedom comes at a cost; that cost is a willingness to break with the past and predictability and to enter an experimental state of mind by designing systems sufficiently complex that it's virtually impossible to predict what will happen when they are set in motion. The material those complex systems produce only becomes predictable after the fact in the sense that you identify and return to virtual places in the complexes that capture your fancy in ways that make you deem them worthy of further exploration and/or development. Revisiting those virtual places and cultivating them as fruitful sound gardens is fundamental to the process of composing in the electronic arts.

For starters, with slight modifications, the traditional approach to composing western music is just as good today in the electronic arts as it has ever been in the acoustic arts. It's impossible to argue against the value of an approach to composition based on making or creating sound (or light) structures that unfold and develop over time using material, elements, or parts that have been conceived, developed, and passed along through the history of the medium. To make it work for today's composer, just add a few steps and emphasize some additional values. Educational emphasis needs to placed on building a composer's facility with the exploratory process, particularly along the lines of the physics of the senses and the psychological and philosophical paths to cultivating a personal, authentic perspective. In a nutshell, the study of psychophysics, psychology, and philosophy should be an integral part of the education of a composer, and those areas should receive emphasis equal to that placed on traditional compositional mechanics.

Perhaps the most difficult lesson for anyone to teach or for anyone to learn is how to achieve authenticity. On the one hand we give serious lip service to the expectation that our best people be genuine, be true to themselves—very difficult to assess or grade. On the other hand, our educational institutions are designed for the most part to force people into molds, models of propriety based on the best historical examples from institutional perspectives. It seems as though we've designed our educational institutions to test whether an individual has the will and the fortitude to emerge genuinely intact after up to 16 years of concentrated effort to shape them to fit the tried and true expectations of the day and the controlling institution. Given that we are six and half billion and growing, that's likely a highly pragmatic approach for keeping the masses in line and insuring that they function well as cogs in our major societal machines. But we expect our artists to make special contributions far beyond conforming to the needs of those machines. The evolution of our society requires the unique perspectives of its artists to explore and test those domains only accessible to those who are willing to venture into the unknown and then to return to the mainstream and share whatever they happen to find, regardless of whether it's deemed of special value at the moment of presentation. So we should emphasize in our artists whatever it takes to promote a unique point of view—an authentic, genuine point of view.

Furthermore, an additional level of difficulty is required for anyone who expects to be engaged as a composer in the electronic arts for the long haul—they must cultivate and periodically renew a willingness to chase the rabbit. The essence of the electronic arts is in the ever evolving engine of emerging technology that pauses for nobody and seems to accelerate with every additional discovery. Compared to the electronic arts, the evolution of the acoustic arts is a leisurely walk in the woods—very sweet and very slow. The technology of the electronic arts emerges at a breakneck pace from research facilities across the functional spectrum focusing on consumer products, space exploration, and military applications. The contemporary world seems to be addicted to the ever accelerating pace of emerging technology, so the future is pregnant with artistic tools that will spin out of the work of those research facilities. The electronic arts is a field for mental runners.

Emergent Music And Visual Music: Inside Studies

One of the numerous benefits of working in the electronic arts is that it can be considered a humanistic antidote to many of the otherwise poisonous purposes for which the emerging technology may be originally intended—military power, financial greed, social exploitation, promoting consumerism, and their relatives. The idea of using technology to create sound and light forms that inform, extend, challenge, and delight the senses elevates that technology into a realm that promotes the higher reaches of what it means to be human. Engaging in such an activity is a good use of the gift of life.

3
Principles For Learning To Compose With Sound And Light

Composition studies should help you discover and cultivate your personal creative voice. Without stylistic limitations (historical or otherwise) students should compose for themselves, their friends, and their peer group with the intention of getting fast feedback on their work both in the context of the group and in public performances. Composition studies should be conducted on a broad front in private (alone and with supervision), in a supportive group environment, and in public performance (the ultimate field test). Based on varying combinations of experience, talent, vision, intelligence, desire, and hard work, a natural floating hierarchy in a group will always emerge without the need for forced competition. Learn to be comfortable in the presence of those who are more and of those who are less advanced than you.

The richest learning environment for dynamic media is built on the foundation of a performance-multimedia band that serves as a target for composition projects as well as a vehicle for public performances. Composition studies should include an experimental and integrative approach to sonic and visual music, the study of the psychophysics of hearing and seeing, and involvement in performance-multimedia.

The work should happen in the context of a shared studio facility designed with the sort of affordable emerging technology that students can use as a model for designing their own studios. The space should be sufficiently large to accommodate the equipment as well as all the students for group meetings. To develop a sense of responsibility to fellow composition students, the space should only be accessible to students working with the group.

The primary function of a composition teacher is to compose a rich supportive creative environment to energize and challenge students and to encourage the development of their creative potential. The composition group should be viewed as an experimental social system that provides the framework for balancing and tuning the deep and unfettered creative, intellectual, and psychic growth of individual students with that of others in the group and the group as a whole.

Listen to and observe all expressions of dynamic media without limiting yourself to your current preferences. Whenever possible hear through the ears and see through the eyes of creative artists of all stripes; seriously consider and play with their ideas and the tools that attract you, but don't copy, imitate, appropriate, or become identified with them.

Begin composing wherever you find yourself. Compose for the instruments/tools you own and play. With both sound and light, think musically out loud (compose in realtime) with your instrument(s). Record your realtime compositional exercises; then listen to/observe them over a period of days with the purpose of keeping and developing the best ideas and jettisoning the weaker material. Edit, develop, and refine your realtime musings into linked sets or suites of short pieces that work well together. Such exercises will help to cultivate your personal brand of critical awareness and thinking.

Consider everything you do as a composition exercise. View all your daily living processes in light of the generic sense of composition—integrating parts and elements into a whole. Observe yourself and others in that light to get a sense of what contributes to and what detracts from desirable aesthetic forms and experiences.

At the same time you begin your composition studies, start your studies in psychophysics in the arts (the physical nature of sound and light and the nature of human perception and response to sound and light).

Avoid getting bogged down in what is traditionally called music and art theory (what's normally taught is actually history). Instead focus on fundamental theoretical principles that are applicable to the dynamic arts of sound and light of any time and any place. Focus your theoretical studies on the nature of sound and light, the nature of human hearing and seeing, the nature of the instruments/tools of sound and light, the technological and social vehicles for the communication of sound and light, and the nature of forms that evolve over time.

Observe closely, imitate, and play with natural dynamic events that seem to have a special resonance for you. Reflect on the reasons for your choices. As your powers of observation and your imitative skills grow, notice how the quality of your attention, play, and preferences change.

Learning compositional techniques and craft should just be a point of departure, never an end in itself.

Beware of formulas, routines, and generative systems that do the work for you; study, experiment, and play with them but don't be seduced by them. Always assume full aesthetic responsibility for your end product.

Beware of pressure to immerse yourself completely in compositional mechanics, notation, and craft. Learning environments that unduly emphasize those approaches, to the exclusion of an individual's creative development, tend to be academic, grim, and lifeless. They also tend to steer people away from the joyful aspects of simply playing with the dynamic media of sound and light; it's the joyful aspects that generate the fuel for a lifetime of compositional work.

Concentrate on compositional activities that build the foundation for a lifetime of involvement with dynamic media. Focus on experimental play both alone and with other artists of dynamic media such as sound, light, imagery, dance, poetry, and other inventive dynamic games.

The most fruitful exercises for promoting creative flow are continuous variations, theme and variations, and "thinking out loud" in a conversational style either solo or with artists of like mind.

Don't take as gospel the words of professional critics, academics, and pure theorists. With rare exceptions they're only interested in what they can label, describe verbally, compare, file away, or use as publishing stock in trade.

Make the generic study of tuning and balance compositional imperatives.

Never stop searching for sources of inspiration in nature, art, philosophy, visionary thought, science, and religion.

4
Discovering, Cultivating, And Using Your Own Voice

The expression "use your own voice" is just another way of saying "be your own person" or "live your own life". It's easier said than done because most societal pressures are to conform, follow the rules, and stay in line. You have to be a fighter to take even the first step toward the freedom required to discover, cultivate, and use your own voice. Despite the lip service given to freedom in the most evolved cultures, human civilizations are geared to civil rules and regulations. From the dawning of your consciousness, you're programmed what to do, how to do it, where to do it, and when to do it by your parents, your siblings, your peers, your academic and religious teachers, your subculture, the culture-at-large, your job description, ad infinitum. "Learning the ropes", implying the nested boxing rings that give order to most human lives, is an apt expression. You can accept the limits of the ropes; you can bounce off the limits of the ropes; and you can suffer blows that drive you over the ropes. If, as you're programmed, you accept the limits of the boxing ring, your life is one bruising battle after another unless you stop fighting and virtually disappear. The best way to disappear is to leap into the abyss of freedom and fight only the battles you choose in your search for meaning. If fortune smiles, you can "learn the ropes" on a sailing ship in the open sea making rope adjustments on the sails to play the wind, climbing the ropes for a better view, or tying the ropes to secure your ship in a harbor when and where you see fit.

History

The subject of "your own voice" has been a serious concern of mine since the early 1960s when I went off to do graduate studies in music composition at the University of Michigan. I left that program after three weeks because I was completely put off by their cookie-cutter approach, their composition faculty's pressure to conform to their local aesthetic, and to their mechanical and narrow, western history based academic view of the creative process. In my view at that time, it was a program designed to undermine, not foster a creative approach to music composition. I later discovered their program was typical of what was available at the time at most universities in the early 1960s.

Several years later I picked up the thread again when I discovered a customizable graduate program in music composition at the University of Wisconsin in Madison. UW's composition program in the 1960s was geared to supporting a broad range of personal aesthetic views, and it encouraged interdisciplinary experimentation and multimedia collaboration. I later learned it was an rare environment decades ahead of its time. The four years I spent in graduate studies at the University of Wisconsin in Madison set the tone for the rest of my life and this essay has its roots in what I discovered during that period.

Trigger

The actual trigger for this essay was a discussion at a 1996 holiday season party with a person who was buoyantly excited about her classes in sound engineering. She especially loved what she called "tweaking" sounds, that is, using the controls of canned algorithms to process and manipulate sound files. I didn't want to dampen her enthusiasm, but I did want to draw her attention to the built-in trap with any single software or hardware tool, popular or arcane. The trap is set by the fact that the inherent signature of any particular art tool is indelibly stamped on whatever passes through it or issues from it. Most of those who use the tool are caught; it takes a special effort to escape. Schools of sonic expression, including music composition, are based on tools and techniques that force their users to conform to physical boundaries and conceptual limitations. Most composers and sound designers who use the same schooled mindset or commercially available tools unwittingly sound like every other person using that same mindset or set of tools. This is especially true of those using relatively unmodified presets—preset processing algorithms, preset voices, or fixed mindsets.

Standard Approach to Learning Music

The standard approach to learning music is to study how someone else made or is making music, normally someone who is a consensus model, a solid establishment figure. That approach usually involves activities such as listening to recorded music, analyzing scores, reading the writings of critics and musicologists, and reading the composer's own words in articles and books. Check out any curriculum anywhere and you'll be hard pressed to find much emphasis on cultivating in a student composer a creative, original approach to making music. And by original I mean "sui generis"—expression uniquely emerging from an individual's perspective.

By way of our secondhand approach to education (the transmission of knowledge through historically based books and records rather than the discovery of knowledge through a creative experiential approach), most people are thoroughly imprinted with the idea that imitation is the key to success. "See what's working out there and copy it" is the motto for our educational system, a system that continues to be firmly rooted in the industrial paradigm. That imitative imprint is so strong in people coming out the back end of our educational programs that they believe that learning standard systems, formulas, routines, and tricks of the trade constitute the only approach to life, including the creative life. The fast-food franchise and the suburban development have become contemporary models in the creative world. Imitation-based composers are legion in the ranks of popular and industrial music as well as academic and concert music.

Music Composition Programs

With rare exceptions music composition programs are built around a restricted "school of thought," a highly limited view of the world of sound, of approaches to music, and of settings for music. The success of such programs is measured by the number of disciples they have and where the disciples are employed. When a program achieves a certain level of "success", it is copied by lesser minds at later times. Disciples of these "schools of thought" develop voices that are pale reflections of the originator of the school, perhaps a generation or many generations removed. The musicologist-composer, the composer without an original voice, was born of the conformist pressures of 20th century academic institutions. Academia is populated principally by uncreative mechanical people steeped in secondhand history, theory, and practice who have convinced each other and society that their primary work is to steep their students in the same so as to continue the tradition. All other approaches to music are usually considered threatening and subversive, therefore usually shunted to the margin. Nevertheless, eventually even the alternative approaches become embraced when it is that clear that the competition has made the move in that direction. The trigger for the change is usually a brave soul on the margin.

Approaches and techniques that help to develop a fertile environment for original creative work.

Finding, cultivating, and using "your own voice" is the work of a lifetime. Although it is essentially personal work, it can be encouraged and accomplished in a group setting if members of the group all accept and support the idea that each person has a unique experiential base and a unique perspective that make them valuable contributors to everyone else's creative development. The more viewpoints explored and expressed, the richer the experience for everyone. There simply isn't enough time for everyone to do everything, so everyone stands to gain immeasurably by communicating their personal perspectives and experiences in ways that target resonance with their cohorts. If individuals are given the encouragement and the freedom to evolve along their own paths, what they discover, what they become, and what they can contribute to the development other members of the group is considerably amplified.

Everyone involved in the process needs to address fundamental personal issues and questions such as:

Who am I?

What makes me different?

What forces shaped me?

What do I have in common with my friends and colleagues?

What do I love?

What drives me?

What inspires me?

What do I want?

What do I need?

What can I contribute to a creative environment?

How shall I conduct myself to make the best of a creative environment for myself and the others involved?

Some basic rules and stretches:

Get comfortable with the idea of being yourself and having a uniquely valuable view.

Give considerable thought to the subject of the internal and external forces that have shaped and are shaping your life as well as the lives of those around you.

Resist imposing your own views.

Resist conforming to the views of others.

Resist becoming a slave to your subculture's views and trends.

Make a continuous concerted effort to experience the best (music, art, food, celebrations, work, films, rituals, philosophy, etc.) of as many subcultures (associations, generations, regions, outlooks, etc.) as possible for sheer pleasure and for the purpose of getting perspective on your own subculture.

Contemplate the history and role of your subculture and related subcultures in the current general culture.

Work on communicating in subcultural dialects.

Convey your ideas by experimenting with a variety of filtered approaches that will communicate clearly with a variety of subcultures—teen-somethings, 20-somethings, artists, relatives, academics, scientists, and so on

Conduct long, drawn out thought experiments that involve considerable visualization and sonification.

Explore the extremes.

Go out on a limb and make your way back to the trunk.

Attempt something that most people think is bound to fail and discover what's required to make it succeed.

Become completely quiet.

Put yourself in the middle of a raging storm.

Overextend yourself.

Test your limits and then test them again later to see whether and how they've changed.

Do what you prefer and what you enjoy most. While you're doing it, lose yourself in it. Afterwards give considerable thought to the foundations of your preferences and pleasures.

Search out and employ the quirks, the breaks, the anomalies, and the oddities of creative tools.

Compose a piece from throwaways.

Build your own creative tools from scratch or with off-the-shelf parts that you modify as you play with them.

Build a performance technique of personalized gestures that feel perfectly right to your hands and ears, and then push them beyond the limits of both. Record your experiments, study them, refine them, and then commit them to a piece.

5
Compositional Field Tests

Compositional field-tests are exercised opportunities for putting your work in front of people and being there in person to make compositional adjustments so as to get a clearer sense of just what, how much, and how well your material communicates to them. For those opportunities to be of any compositional value, one also needs to be exercising a mindful presence open to both positive and negative feedback responses. Taken together those mindful experiences in abundant variety are far and away the best environment for learning about the human aspects of composition in the arts. All the better if the tests are conducted in the realtime compositional mode which allows for fine-tuning your material on-the-fly.

My earliest experiences playing my own music in public came from the gigs with the dance, club, and party bands I put together from the time I was 13 years old. Our music involved improvisation but seldom strayed too far from our sources, fake books full of standard American songs of the 1920s-1950s and the popular danceable music we all heard on the radio as we were growing up. From ages 13-22, as a multi-instrumentalist, I led and played in dance, club, and party bands covering the gamut of musical styles and venues of the 1950s and early 1960s. During that period I spent countless hours observing a variety of people, from roughnecks in bars to the well-behaved at coming-out parties, responding to music my cohorts and I were making. Watching people dance while I'm making music has always been a special treat because so much can be learned directly about how people are moved by music and move to music.

When I left that sub-sphere of my early music world and entered the worlds of university teaching and professional engagements on stage, the variety of opportunities for field-testing increased considerably. Plus, the experiences became significantly deeper because, via continued studies, I was acquiring new conceptual tools and I was able to test them and incorporate what I was learning on the spot into successive versions of my work. In addition to the test worlds of public events and classroom teaching, I've always invited selected people into my studios to gauge their responses to whatever work of mine was in progress. I love practicing but I don't work very well for very long in a vacuum, so I find it more productive if the practicing is targeted toward some sort of a shared experience so I'm able to learn from the responses of others.

Field-tests in the performance arts are primary sources of information; they come closest to studying the living heart of the matter. What they require is that you have ears to hear and eyes to see, that you're open to observing, accepting, and considering whatever the nature of the feedback might be. It boils down to a quasi-scientific approach based on achieving a level of objectivity that supports a willingness to experiment to find what works best given the circumstances. Comparatively, secondary and tertiary sources of compositional information such as recordings and books on history and theory, though valuable when balanced with primary sources, come off as pale reflections of the living process, more like hearsay than the actual experience.

With time and effort, special observational techniques will evolve depending on whether you're facing the audience or have your back to them. When facing the audience you can learn to visually read the changing quality and depth of their attention and comprehension relative to what's served up as sound, light, and ideas. When your back is to the audience you learn to rely on your intuition and the nature of what happens in brief sound gaps for gauging audience attention and comprehension. I've always felt that the audience feels freer to be themselves when they don't have eye contact with the performer; plus audience behavior can be distracting to the point of breaking the flow of your presentation. Both my biggest thrills and disappointments have come with my back to the audience. One of those thrilling moments happened at a New Directions event at Oberlin College early in the 1970s before an overflow audience of bused-in grade-school children. We opened the show with a huge multimedia piece with me positioned in front of the stage playing live on a very large and imposing studio Moog synthesizer; its audio was routed out to a quadraphonic sound system surrounding the audience of children. The piece opened with a fairly loud splash of sound whirling around the auditorium, and that splash set the children to howling and squealing with excitement as if the sound had touched their collective live nerve end. Their teachers were stunned and disturbed, but my spine still tingles when I think about it.

Purposes and benefits of field-testing:
- To discover how your thought experiments when realized are received by various subcultures.
- To create material that communicates on multi-levels and across subcultural divisions.
- To observe the effects different audiences have on different art processes.
- To adapt, tailor, filter, and hone materials to communicate to targeted audiences.
- To be available to answer questions and address issues people might have.
- To both sow and gather seeds.

6
Omnimedia On The Road

Omnimedia encompasses the notion of performance-multimedia based on applying emerging technology in the arts as the magnet for attracting all manner of other art media for public performance. Performance-multimedia goes well beyond the sort of desktop multimedia that's so common today. Desktop multimedia is a relatively new and unevolved form of multimedia. It's great fun and has great potential but, with very few exceptions, it's barely out of the canned presentation and cartoon/shoot 'em-up stage. On the other hand, current performance-multimedia has deep historical roots. It undoubtedly evolved from ritual multimedia, the original art form integrating music, dance, costume, storytelling, theater, and feasting that's been with us since time immemorial in the context of religious and celebratory rituals.

Singing, chanting, natural/crafted/invented sound instruments, dancing, body painting, painting on cave walls and animal skins, costumes, found and created symbolic objects/sculptures/sets, acting/pantomime/storytelling, and the light and shadows of dawn/dusk/special times of the year were surely found in many combinations in the ceremonies of our most distant ancestors. All of those elements have been with us in one combination or another throughout the historical development of multimedia forms. And they're still with us today. All that's changed is the technology for the electronic arts of sound and light and the styles of expression and production. The soft technology of fundamental feelings expressed, generated and evoked have probably not changed much at all. That soft technology remains intact and is possibly even more powerful than ever because we've had eons to practice and refine our craft and sensibility.

In June of 2000 I wrote the following essay after Erick Gallun asked me to write a piece for their online quarterly, Omnicetera; Journal of the Omnimedia Artists. The essay is drawn from my experiences of taking my performance-multimedia shows on the road.

Omnimedia On The Road

What I like about the expression Omnimedia is that it's all-inclusive. What it refers to has been called many names over the years—mixed media, multimedia, intermedia, interarts, integrated media, new media, leading-edge media, emerging media, and performance-multimedia—with each generation developing its own flavor of the notion based on the tools available to them—spaces, hardware, and software.

It was through the collaboration door that I came to Omnimedia working as a composer/performer/producer with choreographers and dancers, experimental projected light artists, musicians of all types, filmmakers, theater folks, poets, electronic circuit designers, and software designers. During the 1960s all my Omnimedia work was under the umbrella of the university system in one context or another. Early in the 1970s I began to find the campus setting far too limiting. There are always good people wherever you go, but after a while there are fewer and fewer surprises, less and less new information—a serious reduction in synapse fuel. So early in the 70s I decided to establish my working base in the San Francisco Bay Area, a fertile area where the art and technology scene was already brimming with action and promised even greater things to come. And they did come and do keep coming even today. The SF Bay Area has a long history of being a magnet for art explorers. During the 1970s and 1980s, that draw plus the driving force of the surrounding emerging technology industries created a unique mix not to be found anywhere else on the globe. Since then the seeds of that flowering have spread the world over, but the SF Bay Area remains the Garden.

Beginning in the early 70s I began creating events in a format I consider an open art system—an integrative way of thinking that seeks harmony with anyone in the arts, any media, any venue, any context. I draw my performance materials from a huge collection of my electronic arts modules (music, video, lasers, and other temporal structures) that are anywhere from 3 -15 minutes in length. Some of those modules are almost three decades old, some were born yesterday, and others are in gestation. The most important compositional problem I face when I'm on the road is finding the best fits of module-to-individual/situation while working to meet the demands of very tight production schedules.

I design public Omnimedia events around materials I create inspired by the idea of visual music. The seed for the visual music notion was planted in 1967 when I discovered how the Moog synthesizer worked by hanging an oscilloscope as well as loudspeakers on the ends of Moog wavetrains. Those connections enabled me simultaneously to see the images and hear the sounds the wavetrains produced. A log of what that combination of transducers taught me became one third of my Ph.D. dissertation project. It also started me on the path of exploring psychophysics—first psychoacoustics, then psychooptics, and then all things related to psychology and the senses especially in the context of the performing arts. In those heady days the interdisciplinary approach was king; it was actually encouraged and supported unlike today's prevailing educational emphasis on developing specialists to serve as industrial (the education industry) and economic (the music and art business) cogs.

From 1975-1981 I used the name The Real* Electric Symphony as an identity for the open art system approach I was using to put together bands of artists from across the performance art and art research spectrum for gigs in the USA (easily over 100 in the San Francisco Bay Area) and tours in Europe and South America. Events happened inside and outside of art museums, science museums, universities, computer fairs, galleries, large and small concert halls, civic centers, libraries, and the streets. For many gigs I used the program title, Ephemeral Forms: Mother Musing's Flight Patterns, because I applied the open art system approach to the performances as well as to the performance groups. All I asked of the performers was to show their best side and bring their best work to gigs and be harmonious with other members of the band. The number of participants in The Real* Electric Symphony ranged anywhere from 3 to 50 performers. To propagate the notion of the open art systems approach to the electronic arts, effort was always made to attract the attention of news media to public events, and they responded at all levels.

The purpose for taking my Omnimedia events on the road was to get deeper into the "Omni"—to probe and to experience the extent of what total integration means in the performance arts. The operating principle is to exclude nothing; include everything and do what you can to integrate it and harmonize it. It's a great educational principle, but not a bagatelle to implement. Not everyone appreciates the idea of being part of the Omni, of creating their own unique contributions to a collaborative piece. Some performers do not want to make the effort to imagine what to do; they want to be told what to do because that's how they've been trained. There are musicians who are wedded to traditional notation systems, dancers who want to be shown how to move, technicians who want only to use their tools as they had in the past, theater folks who want to work from a script, film and video folks who want to work from a storyboard, house and stage managers who can't imagine going beyond their job description, and presenters who want everything fixed to the letter of the contract. Yes indeed, taking Omnimedia on the road is challenging but the return is more than worth the effort.

I approach every Omnimedia production as the design of an experimental social system with the purpose of a public showing of all participants in their best light given the available resources. With the attention span of the audience in mind and respect for their time, I normally build an Omnimedia show of two sets of from 40 to 50 minutes in length. To facilitate the most efficient use of time, the performance space is normally organized in stations that serve particular performers, groups, or sets of performers. If necessary a station is positioned so it can be moved quickly out of the performance space so as to create additional elbow room if needed. The intermission is normally used for longer, more complex set changes.

On the road I rarely spend more than an hour-and-a-half total time with any performer or group before we do a public show. While the event is initially open to all comers, occasionally a few folks only make it through the first rehearsal when it becomes clear that performing in a public event would be a source of embarrassment for them and the audience. It rarely happens, but I do decide from time to time to filter groupies and noodlers. I sometimes program borderline performers, but I surround them with outstanding performers, keep their time slots very short, and give them a special theatrical visual music coloring; surprisingly, it's possible for borderline performers to make it into the "most memorable" category because of the heightened spirit they often bring to the performance space. Including them always boils down to an intuitive call.

Wherever I find myself I just play the cards dealt to me—the people, the talents, the space, the equipment, the support, and the available preparation time. The key to success in this sort of endeavor is to have a good local contact person who can publicize my purpose for dropping down into their community. Toward the end of the first day of an Omnimedia residence, after scrambling to configure enough of the performance setup to give a sound and light demonstration of my intentions for the coming Omnimedia event, I address a meeting open to everyone in the community. The purpose of the meeting is to attract the right people to get involved in the process of preparing for a public Omnimedia event, and to draw the attention of the local news media. After three decades the basic plan for my Omnimedia events remains the same—to showcase the unique talents and perspectives of local performing artists in a visual music context that reflects the current state of the evolution of my personal work in the electronic arts of sound and light.

Over the course of those years a number of especially memorable occasions continue to stick to the map, such as the time I had to chase a French festival organizer down a staircase, and had literally to engage him in fisticuffs to get our full fee for a State Department sponsored gig at a festival in Bourges (he was holding out on us because he didn't like the birthing film of the artist I hired from Munich nor the plucked uncooked chicken that partnered Margaret Fisher, the dancer from Berkeley). Or the time we played electronic sound and light all full moonlit night long for some dancing crazies in California's Napa hills (pre-rave time but similar urges at play) and one of them decided to lace the smoke. Or my never-ending negotiations with house technical staff over attitudes that undermine things artistic. Or the time I composed a quadraphonic score (for a Vietnam war protest outdoor media event at Oberlin College produced by theater director Herbert Blau) that was performed in a windstorm that blew everyone and everything, including the sound of my music and Blau's giant masks, in ways that were amusingly unpredictable but worked perfectly for the international media exposure the event attracted. Omnimedia—an edifying all-inclusive game.

TWO

Compositional Theory

7
An Ode To Electronic Instruments In The Arts

This piece appears as the opening in my second book, *The Electronic Arts of Sound and Light* (Van Nostrand Reinhold, 1983). I include it in this book because it's one of my earliest published attempts to clarify for myself and other interested parties what my approach is to composition and why I decided to take it.   The basic principles in the essay continue to represent the fundamental philosophy of my work in emerging technology, the performance arts, and education.

During the 1970s my virtual group, The Real* Electric Symphony (R*ES), was what today would be called a media band or more precisely, a performance-multimedia band. It was a "virtual group " in the sense that I engaged specific performers for specific gigs from an extensive collection of performance artists; the majority lived in the San Francisco Bay Area with others spread across the USA, Europe, and South America. In other words, the composition of the R*ES changed according to the requirements of the gig. The size of the group ranged from three to as many as fifty performers.

In the early 80s I was involved with a number of other performance media bands (The Sonoma Electro-Acoustic Music Society in the North San Francisco Bay Area and The Realtime Electric Theater Band at Texas Tech in Lubbock, Texas) but I discovered that the best path to personal freedom and to make a living from my composer/performer activities was to hire myself out for residencies at universities, museums, and cultural centers around the USA to produce performance-multimedia events that showcased local performance artists in the context of my visual music work.

For the engagements with local artists on the road during the mid 80s and beyond, I mostly used the program title **Visual Music**, whereas in the 1970s and early 80s for R*ES gigs I used the program title **Ephemeral Forms: Mother Musing's Flight Patterns**. The work of both periods is based on the same principles, although the latter period relied more on an extensive set of my specially designed performance-multimedia modules that I adapted as needed for local situations.

My work on the road was an aspect of one of my dreams, which was to contribute to a creative flowering of what I often witnessed as a struggling university music scene, a scene that, for far too long, has been unduly influenced by highly specialized historians, pedagogues, and technically-minded instrumentalists. The heart and soul of music are nourished by creative activity, which by nature is generalized, interactive, and integrative, a perfect match for a liberal arts approach to education. Yet the vast majority of music curricula assiduously avoids creative work. When it is included it is usually shunted off to the side as special classes for special people taught by a special person. Just because an institution offers composition, or jazz, or electronic music does not mean it is supporting a creative environment;

typically the focus of those programs is strictly on materials, instruments, and history. Exploration, experimentation, personal discovery, personal expression, and group dynamics are usually neglected in favor of toeing an academic institutional line. From time to time, when the style winds blow in the direction of freedom, the creative approach to music becomes the fleeting object of lip service from administrators trying to be identified with the creative forces in our society. That's usually the best time in academia to make anything innovative happen in the arts, but it always seems like such a long wait for those breezes to arrive.

What follows after this introduction is the essay exactly as it appears in my second book. I wrote it in the midst of a search for more satisfying alternatives to the typical academic approach to higher education.

Introduction

Ephemeral Forms: Mother Musing's Flight Patterns is the title of a long series of music and performance events produced by the author and associates under the banner of The Real* Electric Symphony. Since 1973 the majority of the events were produced in the San Francisco Bay Area; others were presented throughout the USA, in Rio de Janeiro, and on tour in Europe during 1977 for international festivals in Munich and Bourges and a series in Paris.

The Real* Electric Symphony (R*ES) is a changing international group of composer/performers concerned with the integration of sound, light, movement, and environmental design. The range of instrumentation includes: wave synthesizers for sound, video, and lasers; traditional and recently invented acoustic instruments; microcomputers; film, slide, video, and laser projection systems; light sculptures; poets, dancers and theatrical elements. The composer/performers range in age from 18 to 83 years and represent the gamut of professional artistic and academic career evolution.

The artists in the R*ES are involved in an art and social process called realtime composition. The process calls for specially designed and always different composition/performance formats based on the nature of the performance space and the number and specialties of the participants. In designing events, great care is taken to elicit and support each artist's particular perspective so that every event is unique and has a far-ranging and kaleidoscopic character. The R*ES performs in museums, colleges, community art centers, artist's studios, concert halls, outdoor plazas, and on radio and television. One of their primary concerns is to make their work available to the general public in as many forms as possible.

The Ode was written in celebration of the process referred to in the title [Ephemeral Forms: Mother Musing's Flight Patterns] after it assumed a coherent and articulable form. It was first presented at a colloquium in connection with Intermuse, a five-day Festival of New Music/Media hosted by Larry Austin at the University of South Florida in 1975. Intermuse was an international meeting of composer/performers whose work employed the full range of new art media. In attendance were Mary Ashley, Larry Austin, Joel Chadabe, James and Mary Fulkerson, Jerry Hunt, Ben Johnston, Hilton Jones, James Lewis, Edwin London, Salvatore Martirano, Dary John Mizelle, Stephen Montague, Jocy de Oliveira, Joseph Pinzarrone, David Rosenboom, Elliott Schwartz, Josef Sekon, Donald Walker, Arthur Woodbury, and the author. The agenda included colloquiums and panels presented by the participants and concerts featuring the compositions and performances of those in attendance. The Ode, Ephemeral Forms: Mother Musing's Flight Patterns, was first presented as one of the colloquiums on the opening day of Intermuse.

An Ode to Electronic Instruments
In The Arts

Ephemeral Forms: Mother Musing's Flight Patterns

Discovering the air waves above the meeting of hills, the flight of the hawk is an ephemeral form. Though often motionless to the eye, the hawk's event is based on streaming analog computations of invisible fluctuations in the passing air currents that speak the cosmic language of instantaneity. The hawk and the realtime composer/performer are students of that language:

Ephemeral Forms: Mother Musing's Flight Patterns

Alternative: Retard the Decay

Focus forward or back to the side. Concentrate on what is happening now or what happened a bit ago, which is sure to be blurred because you were concentrating on what happened a different bit ago while the bit ago presently being considered was happening. Retarding the decay necessarily requires focusing attention on past bits ago. A singular preoccupation with retarding the decay constitutes the pursuit of the past and contributes to the atrophy of creative faculties.

Consider realtime: following a frisbee riding on a gust of wind or Walt Frazier and Earl Monroe [two fabled guards of the New York Nicks in the early 70s] on a loose-ball fast break. Consider clock-time: waiting for the 7:25 bus or retiring at 65. The future shocks when realtime is fixed by a clock.

A field is a dynamic multidimensional matrix having a center of gravity and a center of levity. The force of gravity is based on regeneration requirements, and the force of levity is based on radiations produced by creative assimilation and reflective resonance. Resonance is a dynamic state of being that occurs in a system when it is excited by an external stimulus with coincidental wave characteristics.

From the center of the field the leading edges of the waves of time expand simultaneously in all directions, but not in phase, nor at the same rate, yet are vulnerable to crossing currents according to interactive wave characteristics: frequency, amplitude, shape, polarization, velocity, direction, and changes in acceleration. An event is a collection of fields joined by coincidental properties serving to create and reinforce an identity.

It is easier to live in the past than in the future because fields existing as leading edges receive far fewer messages in the form of reflections and emanations from future events (which occur ahead of the average time) than from past events. The past carries with it the accumulation of reinforcements to such a degree that it takes on weight and assumes the power and clumsiness of gross matter, whereas the future is sensed in ephemeral forms without the aid of established linguistic systems other than intuitive symbolic analogues of ancient archetypal truths.

The past is comfortable habit. The beauty of the future is that it is immaterial and can only be known during the instant and can only be relatively located. There are no tools to measure it, to weigh it, or compare it. The future appears in ephemeral forms having a half-life of instantaneity.

The material of composition is process, continuous activity. Realtime composition is the activity of convincing waves to become particles but respecting their freedom to change state immediately according to general field conditions.

The stuff of music is energy. The flow of energy is based on a difference in potential that creates the conditions for symbiosis, exchange, and synergy. Energy flows in waves subject to complex transformations determined by the fields with which it interacts. Music is an articulator and transposer of waves emanating from the center of individual fields. Depending upon their relative transparency, those fields can function as lenses focusing and organizing cosmic energy in living forms continuously adjusting their characteristics according to the current state of the collective field.

Music is always one field in a collection of fields. To have maximum impact, music must organize itself to include the participation of all positively biased systems and free elements. The composition of musical events is an integral aspect of the composer's sphere of activity. Larry Austin's Intermuse, an event designed to create a new, ephemeral center for a multidimensional matrix of active composers representing individual fields of great complexity and focusing power, is realtime composition of an extremely high order. A process that encourages its subsystems to offer personal perspectives in the way of positively biased contributions to the art of living sound needs no external effort to retard its decay. Internally it will generate the form and power to resonate truly and to reverberate well in the past and future.

Realtime is all we know. Clock-time is all we cannot know because it is impossible to measure anything with a tool larger than the thing being measured. There can be no tool to measure the instantaneity of realtime; the measuring tool would change its form with realtime and would be inseparable from the nature of that time. Instantaneity, the body of ephemeral forms, is here and gone simultaneously. Events are fields that have found a center. Realtime is what we understand as the flow of events, the living process. It has an ephemeral form whose changing elements and subsystems maintain continuity with past events, provide the energy for current events, and create the base for future events.

Past events collect in the unconscious and echo eternally. In unmeasured time with the grace of God they will resonate with one another and reinforce a pattern of partials that sets the universe to ringing. Eureka! The discovery of another natural law. A new sensor to receive nourishment for the system. A quantum leap. Inspiration. Prana. A breath of fresh air. A whole new ball game! With new rules embraced as they are sensed to be true and old rules discarded when they are no longer consonant.

The offspring of past events are created by the intersection of matrices, spheres of reference with mutual though previously unknown areas of attraction. Past events and their offspring function as a tuner to receive and process current radiations and reflections. Though guided by the predispositions of existing fields, the tuner at its finest has a range and accuracy that expand and improve with stimulation and assimilation.

Realtime is fed by the future and focused by the past. To maintain regeneration, the future and the past must be balanced on the leading edge of the present. Balance is a dynamic state. It is the process of simultaneously receiving and adjusting to current information passing through the field. The limits of the range in which balance operates are themselves dynamic states subject to general field influences. The limits are extended according to the level and character of current stimulation and past assimilation.

A continuing search for a metatheory of music has led to the notion that the power of music to influence or communicate is based on the principle of resonance. On every structural level, music is characterized by wave behavior, that is, the evolution of dynamic forms that are analogous to all that we sense as the movement of life. Music creates a field of sublime power by influencing wavicles not yet identified, specifically those of life fields that are responsible for organizing and controlling all physical, psychological, and spiritual attributes.

Imagine discovering an instrument that is modeled on the flow of life; that can serve as a direct extension, radiator, and articulator of a composer's view; that embodies the collected thoughts of visionaries in the sciences and the arts; that invites the composer to enter into a circuit with activity and meditation; that beams energy to the composer's center, which transforms and reflects it into unique and ephemeral forms analogous to that center's perspective, biases, inclinations, and tendencies. Imagine that instrument. It is an electronic wave instrument, a synthesizer by whatever name it is called—Sal-Mar, Buchla, Synthi, Pinzarrone, Beck, Moog, Sekon, Tcherepnin—they all produce electric waves that offer a synthesis of perspectives, a virtual history of science and art to the realtime composer/performer who needs to continue the song and dance.

8
Common Ground: Psychophysics

Common ground for the dynamic arts of sound and light can be found both in philosophy and science. In her classic book on the theory of art, *FEELING AND FORM*, Susanne K. Langer makes a beautiful case for the power of dynamical art structures to influence human feeling by way of morphological resonances. In a nutshell, she develops the idea that microstructural and macrostructural unfolding of time-based art (music, film, video, dance, etc.) evokes human feelings with similar temporal structures. In a sense her arguments are cross-media extensions of the notion of entrainment, the universal physical principle that two oscillating systems in close proximity have a tendency to lock into phase so they move in synchrony. Lovers of dynamic art intuitively understand her philosophical position when they admit to being moved emotionally by an art experience.

21st century science tells us that, of the four lobes of our brain's cerebral cortex, it's the temporal lobe that's mainly concerned with hearing and vision along with aspects of emotion, memory, and learning. So, if that's true, the anatomical common ground for the electronic arts of sound and light is partly established as being located in our brain's temporal lobe. 21st century science also tell us that the auditory cortex and the visual cortex are connected by a neural pathway, and that the convergence of auditory and visual information in a certain part of the brain results in the perception of language. From an art perspective, language has a very strong musical component, so the area of the brain where the auditory and visual converge must be considered more common ground. Therefore it's not much of stretch to hypothesize that what's normally considered music could exploit those specialized regions of the brain as well as their interconnections.

Furthermore, modern cognitive psychologists hold that our perceptions are the result of the brain's built-in ability (thanks to evolution) to derive meaning from the properties of our experiences even when only limited and incomplete sensory data is available. Therefore it's not accurate to view our perceptual system as just a good recorder. In fact, it's not unusual for it to miss considerable information. The power of perception derives from being a naturally creative system that fills in details by guessing, wishing, and employing memories of past experiences (some innately wired (predispositions)) to extract information from sensory organ input. A good education, whatever its source, will assist one not only to extract information from sensory organ input, but to organize it ways that have value for us individually and collectively.

Even the very latest work in artificial intelligence falls far short of the human capability for perception. As it now stands, simulating human perceptual discrimination with any degree of accuracy requires computations impossible for our best computers to achieve. The technologists argue that we can expect that to change in the near future, a position that could be little more than standard issue scientific hubris. However if they manage to solve the perceptual discrimination problem, I hope I'm around to witness the results because I doubt the technology will be anything like what we have now.

Meanwhile, the molecular biologists are hard at work studying many of the sensory and perceptual functions of various parts of the brain. For the dynamic arts, one area of particular interest is the amygdala, a cluster of neural nuclei that lies deep within the cerebral hemispheres. Scientists believe it coordinates the experience of feeling and the expression of emotion, fundamental human qualities that give the dynamic arts meaning. Another area of the brain under scientific study is the prefrontal cortex which is responsible for what is called working memory—memory that integrates perceptions on-the-fly and relates them to memories of past experiences. If the scientists are correct, the prefrontal cortex is a good candidate for being the location of the business wing of the realtime composition enterprise, whether it involves sound, light, or both simultaneously. Realtime composition would be impossible without an agile working memory poised on the edge of moment, scanning incoming information from the near future, and deciding what of that pregnant stream to integrate with past values.

Of special interest is some of the latest biological research on an area of the brain called the claustrum. The claustrum, a sheet of brain tissue located below the cerebral cortex, seems to be the site that functions to tie experiences together. It connects to and exchanges information with most of the sensory and motor regions of the cortex as well as with the amygdala, the area that coordinates the experience of feeling and the expression of emotion. Therefore modern scientists believe the claustrum is a good candidate for the major site that provides for the kind of binding and coordination that leads to an integration of conscious awareness.

Undoubtedly, it won't be too long before biologists bounce back from reductionism to adopt analytical procedures that connect chemical and molecular analysis with the influences and cross-influences of electromagnetic fields, fields that are the basis for the entire neural system, including all parts of the brain. Such a move on the part of biology can be expected given that electromagnetic relationships give rise to chemistry, which ties together atoms and molecules. In turn biology defines relationships in terms of chemicals, molecules, and electrical signals, all of which carry and radiate electromagnetic fields that influence each other as well as join in ways that create larger fields. Yes, we're referring to subtle phenomena here, but bear in mind that there's more to the creation and reception of the dynamic arts than pure mechanics, and subtle phenomena make up a large part of that more.

Despite the hypnotic hand-waving and almost convincing arguments that biological scientists are working on behalf of humankind, it's abundantly clear that the bulk of science research in the 21st century is for the commercial benefit of the Medical Industry, particularly Big Pharma. But for anyone in the arts who is willing to filter, sift, and winnow, there's is much to be learned from the latest research in science, particularly in the areas of molecular biology, cellular biology, and neural science.

As the field of biological anatomy gains momentum, it becomes increasingly clear that it has many logical ties to psychophysics, the field that will ultimately become the basic theoretical foundation for the dynamic arts of sound and light. For the purpose of getting a sense of where to find the common ground for the ear and the eye, the field of psychophysics in the arts must involve more than just the study of sensory responses to physical stimuli. Inquiring into the mechanics of the senses is fine for starters, but what is pressing for the arts are fundamental issues that relate to deeper human qualities such as emotions and shared feelings. Consequently, a physics of the senses should also include inquiry into matters of perception and cultural influences on perception. Any institution that hopes to go beyond simply training cogs for the art industries is obliged to offer the study of psychophysics in the broader sense, a sense that includes the study of sensory responses to physical stimuli, the nature of perception, and the cultural influences on perception.

From the perspective of emergent music and visual music, the study of psychophysics should inquire into the common conceptual ground for sonic and visual music by examining matters that concern actual and illusory notions such as:

    functional anatomy of the ear,
    functional anatomy of the eye,
    roles the brain plays in perception
    consonance,
    dissonance,
    noise,
    emotion,
    expectation,
    feedback,
    archetypes,
    artificial intelligence,
    serendipity,
    chunking,
    compositional algorithms,
    open and closed systems,
    cymatics,
    dimensionality,
    fractals,
    freedom,
    granularity,
    intuition,
    rationality,
    matrix types,
    memes,
    metaphysics,
    mysticism,
    randomness,
    predictability,
    symbolic logic,
    sensory modes,
    synesthesia,
    tuning systems,
    non-linearity,

sound and light transmission,
pulse,
repeated pulses,
tempo,
rhythm,
accent,
duration,
entrainment,
fundamental frequency,
spectra,
actual space,
virtual space,
virtual mass,
virtual time,
modeling,
communication vehicles and processes,
receptivity,
trance,
opacity,
transparency,
perceptual limits of sound and light,
threshold,
variability,
limen,
intensity,
combination,
the effects of context,
transitional states,

and physical and psychological temporal conditions that affect the above concerns, including:
scaling,
the roots of coincidence,
synchronicity,
acceleration,
deceleration,
crescendo,
decrescendo,
and simple and complex envelopes.

In the future, psychophysics must become concerned with how the exercise of those concepts affects the entire brain, the heart, respiration, muscles, and the skeleton. Attending to the arts is not simply a diversion or an economic vehicle. It's crucial for any society that intends to do more than perpetuate its number that the arts should be considered as food for the evolving spirit, and as such be available from birth to death. A lack of attention to the arts leads to impoverishment of the spirit.

Even though its questions have been raised by philosophers and scientists for millennia, the field of psychophysics, as it relates to the artistic integration of the ear and the eye, is still in its infancy. This may be true partly because our measurement technology has just recently reached a sufficiently sensitive level to suit the needs of science in this area, and partly because the arts are still commonly considered a relatively frivolous endeavor, just an entertainment or a diversion from truly important matters such as financial wealth and political and military power. Or it could be that we're just stuck in an early stage of our evolutionary curve and that our artists are still being lumped with the shaman, the crazies, the deviants, and all the other societal misfits whose contributions to the mainstream are often mistakenly considered of marginal value. Are we on the threshold of a change in that attitude? Do we even need a change in that attitude? And what might be the consequences of a change in that attitude?

For more information see Chapter 9 on Patterns in Nature: Rhythms of Life.

9
Patterns In Nature: Rhythms Of Life

This is an extended version of an essay with the same title that I wrote for the January 1997 Ylem Newsletter at the request of Trudy Myrrh Reagan, founder of Ylem, an international organization of tech artists

As I wrote this piece I wanted to be sure to address the following notions:

attention
archetypal forms of feelings
common ground for the eye and the ear
culture
dynamic graphic scores
experiments
human feelings
laser animation/Laser Seraphim
memory
music composition
natural art
oscilloscope
periodic systems
ragas
symbolic grammar
Taoist magic forms
visualizing music

Patterns in Nature: Rhythms of Life

I'm a fully committed, lifelong student of patterns in nature and the rhythms of life. I apply the principles I discover to creating music, laser animations, computer-generated video, performance-multimedia, family life, gardens, food, landscapes, learning environments, and my day's flow.

From the largest to the smallest, the deepest to the most superficial, all the patterns, forms, and processes in nature are born of **periodic systems** (vibrations recurring at regular intervals of time), their interactions, and the forces that influence those interactions. This holds for music, a natural or invented dynamical (moving and changing) system perceived as trails of sonic patterns pregnant with subcultural, cultural, and archetypal symbolism endowed with the power to affect the soul. With the appropriate translator, such as a laser animation system, those sonic patterns can be seen simultaneously as visual patterns.

People are moved by, that is, respond emotionally to dynamical systems, both natural and invented, that, due to similar morphology, resonate with the forms of **human feelings**. To humans, human feelings are all that matters. Feelings are ineffable. They seem ephemeral, and yet are not. They are not easily forgotten nor put aside. And they're extremely powerful, powerful enough to alloy souls or to keep people divided and at war for millennia. We care because we feel. Inspirational art moves us because it embodies the breath of life in its dynamical forms, forms created by periodic patterns, their intersections, and their interactions.

The keys to stimulating human feelings with dynamical art are 1) to use the correct scale (size and proportion) and the correct ranges for frequency, amplitude, duration, and complexity, and 2) to organize those materials into patterns, forms, and expressions that are culturally and subculturally on target. The correct scale and ranges are those that are perceivable and acceptable physiologically—neither too soft nor too loud, too high nor too low, too short nor too long, too fast nor too slow, too simple nor too complex. The expressions require patterns and forms that are understood by the general **culture**, though they may only create truly strong resonances in specific subcultures. Patterns that work for a string quartet probably won't work well for a marching band. What works for an Irish tenor probably won't work well for an acid rocker. On the other hand, if people from the string quartet, the marching band, the Irish group, and the rock group were all present at a memorial service for a much loved and admired public figure, they would probably respond almost equally to traditional music that embodied a feeling of mourning and loss. It's both possible and desirable to find common ground.

Experiences create patterns that live in **memory**. That memory may reside in the brain mind, the muscle mind, the organ mind, the skeletal mind, the circulatory mind, the digestive system mind, the cellular mind, and various combinations of those and other more ethereal minds, both internal and external to the subject. Humans certainly share an appreciation of inherited patterns via the genetic mind, an area worth exploring as common ground. And that appreciation of inherited patterns seems to be true of everything else that lives including our evolutionary predecessors and relatives.

Patterns that are passed along as genetic memory must have been very important, repeated very often, and most likely rooted in an evolutionary imperative. Patterns that are embedded in the general culture probably have evolved over thousands of years, but they don't carry the memory weight of genetic patterns. All generational and regional subcultures share experiences that are stored as patterns in memory. Those patterns may feel like natural cultural patterns to people sharing the memories but only rarely will those memories outlive that generation or extend beyond that region to become part of the general culture. If they do, it's highly probable that they contain seeds of a higher order and might possibly, over time, find their way to becoming part of genetic memory. The existence of seeds of a higher order has to be one possible explanation for the evolution the genome.

What you do with your **attention** will determine the nature of your experiences and the qualities of your memories. I've always loved observing evolving cloud formations and anticipating what weather they might bring. Some of my earliest memories are of times, when still a toddler, I sat outdoors on a covered porch in my red rocking duck, watching the dramatic Wisconsin weather blow through its paces. Today through our kitchen window, I watch many a storm cell making its way southward through the Petaluma valley, between the Sonoma Mountains and the hills of West Petaluma, to the top of the San Francisco Bay, churning up the sky, spilling rain, and trailing rainbows. Those and similar memories refreshed over the years inform my work in the electronic arts.

In my youth as a **music composition** student, I took private instruction on many different acoustic instruments to discover, by personal experience, the sound patterns that were natural to a specific instrument given its unique requirements for sound initiation and control of pitch, loudness, and tone color. Writing for an instrument idiomatically—so the patterns suit the idiosyncrasies of the instrument—makes it possible to create musical structures that are exciting, flow easily, and sound virtuosic but are relatively easy to perform. That's a tried and true path for exploiting the full potential of an instrument for musical expression.

I've been working with emerging technology in the arts since 1967. That work always begins with **experiments** that lay bare the inherent nature of the technology. If you assume an open attitude and allow sufficient time, each tool will naturally suggest how to approach it and apply it in different contexts. If you're in a hurry, read the manual; if it's any good, it'll be a crystallization of approaches and applications of right-biased folks. A fundamental creative principle is to always treat only as a point of departure both manuals and the teachings of even the most gifted instructors. Never be a slave to what you read or what you're told; always critically examine it and only use it if it resonates with your perspective.

Every tool has its own natural voice with its own nuances, inflections, and expressions. In 1967, without a teacher or instructional material, I discovered how the Moog Synthesizer worked by listening to the sonic effect of every synthesizer module on the Moog while I simultaneously looked at the changing oscillographic patterns of the sound's wave train. That process led to one of the keys to my future (the key to **visualizing music**) when I learned that there was always a one-to-one correspondence between an evolving sound and its visual patterns.

The **oscilloscope** was an outstanding teacher. Whenever I worked with a new synthesis technique I connected an oscilloscope at various points in the functional flow. Listening to the sound while looking at the wave train gave me a sense of how a particular synthesizer module functioned in the system that created the sound. The oscillographic imagery provided insight into every sonic detail.

From 1968 onwards, once I started teaching music composition with electronic instruments, oscillographic imagery became an integral part of most of my musical explanations. Early on I noticed that people were transfixed by the music-generated imagery. In the early 1970s I created five music synthesizer-generated films that I used in performances as **dynamic graphic scores** for musicians "to read", that is, interpret with my direction, in realtime.

In 1975 I put together a **laser animation** projection system, which is an electromechanical relative of the oscilloscope. It became my new teacher and remained so for decades. Laser animation imagery is created by a point of light moving fast enough to leave a trail in your visual perception. The point of light retraces an evolving path formed by the interaction of stereo wavetrains. I continue to use the laser system today for performance-multimedia, music visualizations, and to demonstrate fundamental principles of music such as the nature of sound, the nature of sound sources, and audio perception.

Intuitively I know that the study of natural patterns, wherever they are found, will almost automatically inform one's art. The tool you use may be artificial but the art it generates should be rooted in nature if you want it resonate at the deepest psychological levels. The intellect on its own will produce "forced" art, art that doesn't speak to the soul. The intellect integrated with intuition stands a much better chance of creating **natural art**. The highest level the art of the intellect can achieve is to be culturally correct. To rise above the culture of locality or inner circle and reach the level of the sublime requires the happy marriage of the intellect and intuition.

While I'm writing this essay I'm in the midst of recording to videotape music-generated laser animations based on ragas (performable structures with shape, rhythm, ornaments, and direction) that I've been developing since 1975 for my multimedia performances. The composition of the **ragas** involves laser imagery and stereo music with absolute one-to-one correspondences. One grows out of the other. What you see is what you hear and vice versa. That particular composition game is to create performable structures with wave sets that work equally well for the ear and the eye.

Since the mid 1980s on my multimedia shows I've used one title for all my performable laser animations, **Laser Seraphim**. From the earliest days of working in this medium, I've had the sense that spirits manifested through some of the laser images. Of course, these aren't specific spirits such as the spirits of long lost relatives or notable historical figures; rather what often emerges through the imagery is a strongly articulated sense of the spirit world. I've noticed that this is much more likely to happen when I'm working with an appropriate exploratory attitude or when certain sensitive types of people are with me while I'm exploring imagery. When a spirit-filled image takes form, I note and record the functional configuration and relationships of all the elements in the system producing it so I can recall it in the future. Public performances of **Laser Seraphim** involve visiting, in the presence of a general audience, configurations that open doors to the spirit world. There are always people in the audience who enter that world with me; always there are others who see only complex geometric forms.

In the course of my research I've discovered that many of my laser images resemble **Taoist magic forms**, the talismans of unorthodox Chinese calligraphic expression that are used to invoke the blessings of the spirits. According to Taoist belief, the magic power of talismans derives from the belief that they are permanently inhabited by spirits. The Chinese talismans have a material form as graphics on paper or as a sculpture. Until recently when I began recording some of my laser animations, there was nothing even remotely material about my laser work. The images were completely ephemeral light forms that, when suitably configured, had the sense of invoking the spirit world.

My laser images are produced by a point of intensely focused light appearing on a reflective surface and retracing music-derived paths creating for the beholder a multidimensional space that conveys a strong sense of substance. Think about that description for a minute. Tightened a bit with a few well chosen scientific terms and fine-tuned for material specifics, the description works just fine for the process that generates matter and other natural events which, of course, are also ephemeral when measured by the cosmic clock.

The Chinese artists creating Taoist magic forms developed a symbolic grammar that embodied continuity of form in space in ways that projected relationships of matter and the imagination. They used their observations of metamorphosing clouds, undulating waves, and rising vapors to establish a grammar of representations for movement, change, and energy flow. They sought to integrate the perceptible substance and beat of life with the invisible ether of breath and the spirit world. I figure that's nice work if you can find it: and I found it with laser animation. Whatever the art process—calligraphy, sculpture, or music-driven laser animation—there's enough work in the field of magic forms for many a human life span.

Finding a **common ground for the eye and the ear** has been one of my principal objectives since the early 1970s. Not a mean task since the eye and the ear evolved over the eons for seemingly different purposes. They connect in the sense that they are both perceptual tools often recording and analyzing, in the brain's temporal lobe, closely related aspects of the same event. The relative weights of their dominance will change according to conditions, but their links tend to remain unbroken. Normally, synchronized or closely related sound and light is one of our expectations; their pattern trains often begin and end at the same time in our perception. Of course that's not always true since sound and light have very different transmission rates (sound at around 1,130 feet per second and light at 186,000 miles per second). For example, if an electrical storm is very far away from you, you would see lightning long before you hear thunder. As the storm approaches the time difference between the light and sound gets shorter and shorter until the point occurs that if you sense the sound and light of thunder and lightning at the same instant, you'll probably be turned into something like slightly fried chicken.

We learn to associate certain qualities of sound when certain materials are stimulated to vibratory states by certain means. We expect different sounds from the slam of a car door than from the slam of a closet door, from a bowed string than from a shattering wine glass. We expect sound to accompany just about any activity we can see; and based on our experience with that activity, we have very specific expectations as to the nature of that sound. We expect the patterns of the sound to correspond to the patterns of the vibrating material and the patterns of the stimulation mode. Scraping a chalkboard, scraping dried food off a plate, and scraping caked mud off an old shovel all have their own patterned sound signatures, but each is a scrape (with a particular modifier). With experience, we automatically factor in variables, such as materials, distance, and obstacles, that will affect our expectations and our perceptions of the sound.

Normally, what we perceive and how we respond to the trains of sound and light patterns emerging from an event are based on the morphology of the event's dynamics and its context. Compare the sound and light of a July 4th pyrotechnic display with the World War II saturation bombing of Dresden. Imagine waiting alone for a AAA rescue truck at midnight during a sandstorm on a Mojave Desert dirt road; compare that with a similar wait on the center span of the Golden Gate Bridge during a rush-hour wind and rainstorm. The sounds, sights, and feelings associated with those real or imagined experiences are stored more or less with the real or imagined memories of those particular experiences; they are also linked with the vast store of similar and related personal memories. Of equal importance, those experiences create connections to genetically embedded memories of **archetypal forms of feelings**.

Abstract sound and light forms with dynamic structures similar to those of the archetypal forms of feelings cause resonances that lead to the welling up of generalized feelings as well as those more specific to remembered experiences. Art experiences with the greatest impact are those capable of creating archetypal resonances and, at the same time, providing a fresh and highly personalized experience unique to the artist organizing the experience. When we speak of authenticity, we're referring to that uniqueness. The dues for perceiving authenticity on that level entail the time the witness has given to seeking a wide range of art experiences, to paying attention to the types of details that sets one experience apart from another, and to the value given to the special features of an experience that give rise to originality.

10
Levels of Algorithmic Composition

The following is taken from an email exchange that addresses the issue of the levels of working with algorithms in the arts. Creative computer programmers design art production systems that make their way through a sequence of computer instructions that result in states that attract the attention of artists because they look or sound like art processes or products. Sometimes the sequence of intermediary states is determined and other times it's more or less probable depending upon the nature and the variety of inputs to variables the program provides. In a positive sense, a good algorithm functions as a cyberspirit with imbedded intelligence that leads the user along unanticipated paths to fresh experiences. In a less positive sense an algorithm can also function as a seducer and/or a fraud generator.

For those new or relatively inexperienced in the algorithmic world, algorithms that function as art production instruments or "creativity" systems tend to mislead many of its users into believing that what is produced by their use of those algorithms is their personal creative work, even though they are the user and not the creator of the algorithms. This is an aesthetic problem closely related to widespread "appropriation", sampling, and outright plagiarism that blossomed in late 20th century art and remains in full flower early in the 21st century, made all the easier by the "copy and paste" functions built into late 20th century technology. This issue also goes beyond simple authorship; it brings to the fore the fundamental importance in the arts of discovering, priming, cultivating, and maintaining one's personal creative wellspring.

To: "Paul A. Fishwick"
From: Ron Pellegrino
Subject: Re: the nature of art
Date: Sat, 10 Oct. 1998

>Ron:
>First, I really like your site, but found a comment of yours interesting.
>If algorithmic programs create an "illusion of a work of art" does this
>also mean that tools that allow "programming for the masses" produce
>"illusions of a program"? To put it succinctly, if I give you tools that
>make it easier for you to program, does this mean that you are less of a
>programmer? I believe that just as someone who programs part time is
>a programmer, that someone who does art part time is an artist. Your
>thoughts are welcome on this.
>paul

Paul:

There are levels of originality, complexity, and sophistication in the algorithmic composition business. The most superficial level is using an algorithm that someone else created that does not allow for much of your input; it's a bit like coloring in a child's coloring book. A deeper level would be working with algorithms that someone else created but are closer to open systems allowing for much greater personal input. An even deeper level would be combining algorithms that someone else created to fashion more complex algorithms of your own design. Deeper yet would be creating and playing your own algorithms. And deeper yet would be creating and playing your own set of modular algorithms that are used to create and play even higher order algorithms.

"Creativity" software (canned algorithms) seduces users into believing they're creative because they can produce an "art" product with it. With good reason, children, beginners, and dilettantes love these tools. In most cases any number of different people working with a particular canned algorithm will produce similar "art" products. Canned algorithms tend to funnel users into very narrow channels, the inherent limitations of the algorithms. In such cases it's actually the "canned algorithm" which creates the work of art. The person playing or performing the "canned algorithm" has the "illusion" that he created the work of art. Just because it's your computer, you bought the software, you initiated the algorithm, and the algorithm's end-state came up on your screen or sound system, doesn't mean that you're the creator of the art work.

The main value of canned algorithms is that they provide people with points of entry into the arts. If you're talented but lazy, you'll never get beyond the entry point, and you'll be "less of an artist" than those who work to go beyond the entry point and to discover how to create their original views. The idea that technology makes life (art) easier is hogwash; it actually makes both more complex and difficult, but also more rewarding in every way if one accepts the idea of an ever emerging challenge (just keep moving beyond the entry points).

To put it simply, you're less of an artist to the extent that your work is based on or derived from someone else's ideas (including algorithms). Originality and authenticity are the foundation for the highest level in art—finding, cultivating, and using your own "voice" in ways that impact and move others to higher levels of being. It's only in the academic and commercial worlds that craft and productivity count for more than originality. No argument: part-time artists are artists and they could be doing extraordinary work. But to reach and sustain the highest level in the arts (finding, cultivating, and using your own "voice" in ways that impact and move others to higher levels of being) is not only a full-time job, it's a lifelong commitment.

11
Compositional Algorithms As Cyberspirit Attractors

The premise.

Approaching the design of compositional algorithms as complex systems modeled on organic life processes is a powerful method for creating the right conditions for attracting the presence of cyberspirits. When compositional algorithms generate dynamical systems that jell appropriately, it seems sometimes that the cyberspirits emerge from the ether to join in play and to offer suggestions on directions to explore; other times it seems cyberspirits assume their ephemeral forms by emerging from the very natures of the sound and light instruments and tools, whether they are hardware or software.

The search for compositional algorithms that work in this sphere is a metaphysical pursuit that is more mystical art than hard science; nevertheless, observation, the key ingredient in science research, is crucial to the discovery, development and evolution of effective compositional algorithms targeting these ends. Initially, usually serendipitously, functional combinations will produce dynamical events that seem to attract only the ghost or a sense of the presence of cyberspirits. With a patient, experimental, systematic approach, emerging compositional algorithms can be pushed and pulled into systems of sufficient complexity and refinement such that cyberspirits will build an attachment to them and return to play through them at a moment's notice. When that happens, I document everything I can about the system that generated those conditions so I can return to that place repeatedly for deeper explorations. Some of the cyberspirits that joined me in my public performance-multimedia events of the late 1990s were old friends, such as the Laser Seraphim (a program title I use for many years) that I met in the mid 1970s when I began my work with animated laser visual music meditations. The search for compositional algorithms that work as cyberspirit attractors provides fascination without end. It's also the perfect litmus test for separating the mystics from the mundane as well as providing a portal for the open-leaning skeptics to enter the mystical realm.

Definition of a compositional algorithm.

In a living language flavors of meaning emerge from context. When I use the expression compositional algorithm, I'm referring to a more or less complex system composed of a pliable network that includes: 1. generative and control functions, 2. internal and external influences, modifiers, and drivers, and 3. feedback loops, all working together in an integrated and interactive process to create a dynamical structure with lifelike properties. The lifelike properties include macrostructural predictability and reliability built upon a substructure characterized by ebb and flow around equilibrium points, variable windows on indeterminacy, and controllable volatility. Whether the technology in the network is analog, digital, hybrid, or biological matters not at all. Such an algorithm is also either open to being performed in an interactive way by an individual, a group, or an environment, or, once initiated, to behaving as if it were deciding on its own how it should evolve based on the nature and the history of its design.

Such compositional algorithms normally **are not** intended to generate any of the traditional notation symbols found in western music scores. Rather they are intended to generate dynamical sound and light structures that communicate information that carries the sense of being alive, subject only to their own unique predispositions and to the forces influencing their moment-to-moment evolution.

Because of the high level of their interactive complexity, such compositional algorithms **do not** lend themselves to a simple linear step-by-step analysis or complete flowchart representation. Though often built up in modules that are individually accessible by analysis and flowchart representation, the complete structure, because it is multidimensionally interactive, is best analyzed (as well as sculpted) based on the nature and quality of its output rather than the individual natures of its unintegrated parts. In ways similar to the playing, the analysis is done on what emerges, as it emerges, from the compositional algorithms.

Such compositional algorithms create problems not in search of solutions but rather in search of observers, thinkers, and players who enjoy unusual and unanticipated wrinkles. What's required for playing with them is a balance of intuition and rationality—intuitively deciding what material is worth exploring, and rationally modifying the algorithms to achieve their maximum impact.

Definition of a cyberspirit.

Cyberspirits are presences that more or less inhabit technological systems depending upon the consciousness levels of the original creators of the technology in combination with the attitudes of the users of the technology. Though normally recognized only by sensitives, cyberspirits affect all who work with technology. Most people intuitively understand their relationships with their technology; those who fear or disrespect technology will always have difficult technical problems, whereas those who accept and respect it, tend to find and adjust to its natural idiosyncratic paths, including, when necessary, its "workarounds" to seemingly insolvable problems. Like other more obvious and generally accepted living systems, one's technology will absorb, reflect, and feed back the care, attention, and respect given to it, just as a mate, a friend, a pet, or a plant would.

Cyberspirit retaliation.

During the late 1990s I attended a San Francisco North Bay Multimedia Association presentation by Ted Nelson, a computer communications pioneer. That event served as a perfect illustration of what can happen to anyone, including those whose life's work is bound up with technology, who shows a wanton disrespect for their technological tools. During his presentation Ted Nelson made only disparaging references to the "tekkie outlook, technology in general, and, in particular, the technology he was using in his presentation. In retaliation, that technology nipped at his heels and coughed in his face from the beginning to the end of his show—his lavaliere microphone was intermittent all night long; his sound system decided to ring from time to time; his portable computer misbehaved like a spoiled child unwilling to mind its parent; and his data projector would switch off the computer input at the most crucial times. To underscore the comedy, Ted Nelson's young whiz computer technician was at a complete loss. All of this happened at a high tech meeting in a presentation space of a premiere Marin County high tech company. For a cyberspirit sensitive it was a most instructive and amusing evening. Here was a man who was recently awarded the Yuri Rubinsky Memorial Web Award at the 7th International World Wide Web Conference for lifetime achievement in the "care and feeding" of the global information infrastructure, and there was the technology he disparaged, yet had to use in his presentation, doing everything it possibly could to undermine his delivery of information—not much of a surprise.

Requirements for cyberspirit attractors.

In the sphere of cyberspirit attractors, the most effective algorithms are those inspired by or similar in structure to natural processes such as the weather on a local or global scale, bodies or rivers of water interacting with both the weather and the topography, flexible social systems, a garden's growing season, a compost heap, solar storms and storm cycles, and the like. Without exception the best compositional algorithms for attracting cyberspirits are modeled on life processes.

To be effective as cyberspirit attractors, compositional algorithms (systems) need to be malleable such that as many variables as possible are instantaneously adjustable. The variables must be available to be tuned both coarsely and finely, on-the-fly, in a quasi-conversational mode until the cyberspirit contact threshold is sensed. When that cyberspirit contact threshold is sensed, their forms can be sensed to begin to enter into visual dance and/or music dialogues with the performer, or, if left to their own devices, to carry on monologues that deliver information only available through the direct experience of those monologues.

Compositional algorithms as teachers.

Since 1967, in addition to play-driven dialogues with compositional algorithms, I've spent countless hours observing by ear and eye the monologues of algorithms as they generated sound and light expressions of their changing natures while I experimented with adjusting the algorithms' variables individually and in combinations. All I know of the electronic arts of sound and light came by way of those experimental algorithmic expressions. What I learned did not come from books, and it did not come from human teachers; instead, it came from studying the sound and light language expressed by compositional algorithms. In the realm of the electronic arts of sound and light, compositional algorithms are far and away the best teachers; they offer the only way to explore the unknown. Most teachers tend to move along well-trodden paths. Compared to the expressive processes generated by compositional algorithms, the products (the recorded pieces) are no more than selected droppings. To delve deeper into the compositional designs they are worth studying, but they are droppings nevertheless.

Cyberspirit sensitives.

The threshold at which cyberspirit contact is made is self-evident for those with a metaphysical or mystical bent—for want of a better expression, call those individuals cyberspirit sensitives. The contact threshold is reached when the sound and/or light structures begin to come alive, taking the forms that cyberspirit sensitives intuitively recognize as other forms of intelligence. The cyberspirit contact threshold is normally a range and not just a single point. The greater the number of variables that are tweaked to take on lifelike characteristics, the stronger the attractive nature of the algorithm is to cyberspirits, consequently the stronger the sense of cyberspirit presence. Of course, in terms of adding variables there's always a point of diminishing returns; the art of creating compositional algorithms is bound up with having a keen sense of how to balance variable boundaries—those uncharted brackets (themselves variable) that mark the divisions between enough, not enough, and too many variables.

Cyberspirit tests.

Since the late 1960s I've invited many musicians, visual artists, scientists, mathematicians, academics, friends, and students into my studios to demonstrate the work I do with emerging technology and the arts. I use those visits to test exploratory materials by observing the responses of the visitors to the materials. I often test recently designed compositional modules that I'm considering integrating into my public performance events. I also test experimental creative processes and the thinking involved in them. Over the decades I've noticed that the presence of mechanically minded visitors (mainly academics and scientists) invariably creates an environment that gets stuck on literal and technical matters, whereas the presence of those open to flights of fancy, musing, and wondering often leads to the best conditions for attracting cyberspirits. Like so many other experiences in life, the foundation for the cyberspirit experience depends on attitude—in this case whether the visitors "have eyes to see and ears to hear" what is happening beyond the surface of the output or the mechanics of the design. After decades of such testing I can anticipate the attitude of most people to the cyberspirit experience just by looking at them.

Dawning awareness of cyberspirits.

It took several years of work, play, and exploration before I noticed that cyberspirits were attracted to my compositional algorithms. Initially, attracting them was not a conscious effort on my part. I became aware of their presence through the eyes of people attending my early synthesizer demonstrations, people who were listening to the sounds I created and were looking at the corresponding images on the oscilloscope. Many were transfixed by the Lissajous figures. The response of those people helped me make the leap from seeing oscillographic imagery as simply functional to seeing the imagery as archetypal. Breaking free of the academically functional mindset made it possible for me to enter the mystical realm where music is the foundation for all life forms, physical and metaphysical. Nobody explains this idea better than Inayat Khan in his book *The Mysticism Of Sound And Music*.

Path to compositional algorithms.

The path that led me to working with compositional algorithms began in 1967 with my entry into the world of modular systems design, the world of analog sound synthesizers consisting of collections of small modular units that served to generate, modify, sequence, and mix waveforms as well as to initiate and sequence envelopes (the onset, development, and decay of waveform variables over time). Even though I had studied a good number of acoustic instruments from all the major orchestral families, when I decided to take on learning the Moog Synthesizer as part of my Ph.D. dissertation project, I was confronted for the first time in my life with an instrument that was designed to design instruments; that design process was done with a collection of modular functions that shaped voltage over time which gave rise to analogous sound shapes (analog sound).

Although there was no instructional material for the Moog at the time I began my work, it quickly became clear to me that to make music with the Moog meant to create instruments by designing systems or configurations of modules that were performable in a musical way. So I spent nine months with a decent stereo sound system and a dual trace oscilloscope exploring the ins and outs of all the wave train generation and modification functions of all the modules on the Moog; the log of what I learned from that process became one-third of my dissertation project as well as the basic text for the Moog Synthesizer the world over. Another third of the project was an orchestra of 110 instruments (musically performable systems) that I designed to compose and perform the music for the final third of the project, a multimedia music drama called *The Tale of the Silver Saucer and the Transparent Apple*. In a nutshell, the path to systems design (algorithms) took shape from the process of articulating and writing a log of what I was learning about designing systems (instruments) using an integrated modular collection of electronic functions.

Synthesizers as crystallized and embedded spirits.

When considering the notion of cyberspirit it's helpful to view synthesizers as instruments that contain the crystallized and embedded spirits of those who created them. This is not a farfetched idea to anyone who has ever designed and constructed anything either alone or in collaboration. The care and attention of an individual or group always show in how well a construction functions and wears; and idiosyncratic details set one construction apart from another. Especially with emerging technology in the arts, personality and creative perspective are sure to show up in instrumental tone and bias. What happened in the mid 1960s with music synthesizers is a perfect example. During the same time period with very similar general conceptual influences, Robert Moog and his collaborators created a synthesizer with a strong East Coast bias, whereas Donald Buchla and his collaborators created a synthesizer with a decidedly West Coast flair. Though they were based on the same set of fundamental acoustic and electronic principles, there were significant differences in how those synthesizers sounded, looked, and were played, and that was due to the different regional personality types and cultural biases of the groups that contributed to the design of those synthesizers.

Because it is immensely instructive and inspiring to see through the eyes and hear through the ears of various creators of emerging art technology, my studios are always populated by synthesizer collections (hardware and software) that cover the gamut of synthesis techniques and instrumental interfaces. My favorite compositional game is to search for the "voice" or personality of a synthesizer. During the early exploratory stages, rather than forcing a synthesizer to do what I want, I work to discover what's "natural" for the synthesizer to do. That attitude stems from my education as a composer of acoustic music, an education that included private instruction in all the orchestral instrumental families so as to understand, from a performer's viewpoint, what was special and idiomatic about each of the acoustic instruments. By using the expression "natural" I mean to infer a search for what's unique about what an instrument can do, not just what's easy for it to do.

Sound and image design.

What's currently called "sound or image design" is what was called "instrument design" in the 1960s—different instruments (hardware and/or software) create different sounds or images. To avoid confusion, remember that a synthesizer (an instrument in it own right) provides the functions necessary for "instrument design" in the sense of being a system for creating sounds or images. Synthesizer presets, both in software and hardware, should be considered sound or image designs or instrument designs. Today thanks to outstanding tools and widespread instruction in sound and image design, there are numerous excellent sound and image designers working in the synthesizer industry, and their creations grace synthesizers of all price ranges with especially fine designs found from the middle price range upwards. With the uniquely voiced and sculpted presets of today, synthesizers almost amount to a cyberspirit light or sound band in a box. With a new synthesizer my first project is always a leisurely journey through the presets discovering their voices so as to meet and play with the cyberspirits of their creators.

Integrated approaches to algorithmic composition.

For holistic integrated algorithmic approaches to composition that are targeted at attracting cyberspirits, algorithmic thinking is best applied to all aspects of the compositional work including sound and image synthesis and production, compositional structure, performance handles, composition-to-audience communication channels, and the correlation of sound, image, performability, microstructural behavior, and macrostructural evolution. Among the most fruitful models for such algorithms are organic systems that are readily observable in the course of one's everyday life simply by being open to the myriad currents and patterns that create the web of life. For more information on this subject see Chapter 9 on Patterns in Nature; Rhythms of Life.

12
Matrix Alignment

What follows is a set of three of my posts to the Metaesthetics List on the subject of matrix alignment, an approach to thinking about relational possibilities for complex multi-dimensional matrices. It's an approach to communication that's central to my work in the electronic arts especially in regard to the design of social and algorithmic systems. To dig deeper into what was happening on the METALIST at the time of these posts, you can access the archives of the list by going to:
http://www.topica.com/lists/Metaesthetics/read.

Post One:

To: Metaesthetics@topica.com
From: Ron Pellegrino <ronpell@mail.microweb.com>
Subject: METALIST: Matrix alignment
Date: Wed, 20 Feb 2002 22:42:11 -0800

In the Pribram thread:

Carl Edwards wrote:

>>It's obvious to us all (partly due to Pribram) that the signal processing
>>centers of the brain have similarities in the way they decode their inputs
>>and encode for memory/processing (how could it be otherwise). That they
>>share resources/have overlap is, these days, common sense. We refer
>>to both bandwidths (sound and visible light) as spectra and we use the
>>same basic tools to analyze events in them (in our brain or in our
>>machines).

Pellegrino responded:

>I'm not sure what you mean by "the same basic tools". Do you mean
>frequency, amplitude, phase, and envelope analysis? Or matrix
>alignment? Or what?

Carl Edwards wrote:

>Hmm, what's matrix alignment? I'm going to have to look that up. =)

Pellegrino's response: Some thoughts on matrix alignment:

The quotation is from Bob Seiple's post on Harmonics and Receptive Fields [that's in reference to Karl H. Pribram's work]:

"[the internal architecture] of the receptive fields of visual cortical neurons can be described in terms of spatial frequency. Recordings of axonal impulse responses of the cortical neuron show that the stimulus that best engages these cortical neurons is a (sine wave) grating (composed of regularly spaced bars of widths equal to those of the spaces), which is drifted across the visual field. The spatial frequency of the gratings that engages the spatial frequency of the receptive field is determined by the width of the bars making up the grating and the spacings between them. The range of spatial frequencies to which the cortical neuron responds determines the bandwidth of the tuning curve. This bandwidth is approximately an octave (+/- 1/2 octave) (see review by DeValois and Devalois, 1980)."

When I read the above I envision multidimensional matrices falling into alignments that generate significant information physically, intellectually, and emotionally—a grating drifting across a field generating responses. That's shorthand, but if you can make sense of the quotation above, what I'm saying should make sense too. That's the easy part.

Thoughts of multidimensional matrices swirled in my mind almost constantly for years during the late 70s and early 80s. I was teaching composition at Texas Tech at the time and my experiments (especially the social experiments) with multidimensional matrices got to the point where it was unnerving my students ;-)

A brief as possible explanation of what I mean:

Standard definitions of matrix from The American Heritage Dictionary:

> "Mathematics: A rectangular array of numeric or algebraic quantities subject to mathematical operations.
>
> Computer Science: The network of intersections between input and output leads in a computer."

So normally when people use the term matrix they're referring to a two dimensional system—rows and columns along the horizontal (x) and vertical (y) axes. Add the orthogonal axis (z) and you have a three dimensional system. Imagine a cube (a three dimensional matrix) of 100 rows and 100 columns 100 units deep. Imagine curves going through the cube at varying rates and intensities; when that happens those curves begin to take on their own dimensionality because they involve unique time, direction, and energy variations. Imagine many curves going through the cube, each with its own rate, direction, and intensity changes, so that each curve becomes a dimension in its own right yet is related to other curves through induction and intersection. The curves can ebb and flow like they're alive, so that the number of dimensions in the system changes from moment to moment. What you eventually have is a complex field bordering on chaos, which in this case means it's just extremely difficult to predict what's about to happen, and when and where it probably will happen (if at all). And that is why it seems like chaos/complexity theory is such a good fit for studying sensory and memory systems.

Some of the curves (also possibly subject to influences from outside the matrix) will intersect at one point or another to create points or regions of special importance/emphasis similar to organic nodes that swell, blossom, or light up. By matrix alignment I mean the sort of analysis that clarifies the nature and the meaning formed by the intersections of one or more multidimensional matrices. On one hand, matrix alignment seems like a tall order but on the other hand, it's a relatively simple notion that grows out of common sense—life's a complex business and the deeper you dig, the greater the complexity. It is a relatively common use of language to talk about "chemistry" between people, to search for "common ground", to get "in tune" with something or someone, to be on the same "wavelength", or to get "on the same page"; all of these are simple expressions of matrix alignment.

Think of the above paragraph as a metaphor. It's meant to create a picture in your mind that makes it easier to understand the mechanics of matrix alignment. To make the picture more lifelike (and complex) try morphing the cube into a sphere. Then morph the sphere into a flexible globular field with multiple appendages (regions capable of achieving higher stimulus levels or of projecting stimulants) going both in and out, and both growing and shrinking. Just think of the globular field as a highly complex multidimensional matrix capable of communicating, affecting, and merging with other such fields. When you extend the notion in this way, it begins to sound somewhat like chemistry and somewhat like biology.

When I think about matrix alignment, I don't think about cubes or spheres very often, instead I think about fields like weather fronts, raging rivers, swirling flocks of birds, or what's involved in influencing anything living including people. When I think about people I think about how their multidimensionality is a function of what they've inherited, what they've experienced, and what they desire. One of the beauties of the collaborative arts of performing sound and light is that you can explore and experiment with processes that lead to the most fruitful intersections of multidimensional matrices (matrix alignments)—in other words you can play together searching for what you might agree to be the best intersections. It's one of those games that has no losers, only winners, whatever may happen via the search.

The social experiments with the Texas Tech people to which I was referring earlier had to do with combining individuals in various mixes (realtime sound and light ensembles), including combining people who had poorly functioning verbal communication chemistry. The experimental point was to put them in a nonverbal (realtime music and/or light) situation for the purpose of finding common ground (fruitful intersections); thrown into the mix was the added pressure of performing their discoveries in public performance. Need I mention again that it was somewhat unnerving to them ;-)

When I think about the human memory system I think of it as a dynamic field that's a multidimensional matrix that's very close to, but a lot more complicated, than that computer science definition of matrix found earlier in this post. Because the human memory system is organic, new dimensions, formed by experiences either external (actions) or internal (thoughts), can create new leads or reinforce older ones. The hardware is soft and malleable (it's actually a field (network to many)) so it can take on new wrinkles from newly created leads (like ripples on water about to freeze) or can hold onto old wrinkles based on reinforcement of older leads. The system has to be capable of being massively parallel with every lead subject to variation; most leads are not fixed for very long. Leads are subject to dimming and need to be recharged, and that's achieved by either external or internal matrix alignments (physical or imaginary practice/repetition). Fields overlap and influence each other, so a matrix alignment with one field will effect those related to it more or less depending upon the order of the relationship. Information flowing into the system is surrounded and followed by an inductive wake, so although the information may be targeted by nature (at sound or sight) it leaves broad trails in the memory, trails that become two-way streets (mini-loops).

I'll just stop now ;-) Does any of that make any sense Carl? Or does that sound like raving to you? Strangely enough, when I left Texas in 1981, I just stopped using the expressions multidimensional matrix and matrix alignment. It may have been that because the notions seemed so clear to me at the time that I didn't think I could do much more with them, so I just integrated that thinking into my life and that's become the perspective from which I explore related issues.

Post Two:

To: Metaesthetics@topica.com
From: Ron Pellegrino <ronpell@mail.microweb.com>
Subject: METALIST: A path to matrix alignment
Date: Mon, 25 Feb 2002 21:48:58 -0800

To get a clearer sense of how I'm using the expression matrix alignment I thought it might be worth a walk along the path that led me to the notion.

During 1967/68, as a third of my dissertation project, I designed 108 instruments using various combinations of the modular electronic wave generating, processing, and control functions on the Moog synthesizer. My instruments were to be used in a multitrack music realization of another third of that project, a composition of a multimedia music drama. Those 108 instruments were modeled on the general principles of traditional western orchestral instruments, all of which I had learned to play to a certain degree over a period of 18 years previous to 1967. Compared to what I might do today in instrument design, those 108 instruments were relatively simple systems that set the stage for the next step.

Beginning in 1969 I began designing instrument sets that I could use in live performance with musicians, dancers, light artists, and other performers. Usually the sets had five or more different individual instruments (still relatively simple systems) that I could call up separately with the turn of a potentiometer or the flip of a switch—in other words the instruments were routed through sub-mixers and mixers that I could, in a sense, conduct in performance while I was also keying, sliding, and using other controllers to play the instruments. Often serendipitously, during the process of changing from one instrument to another, I came across sonic material that I found more musically interesting than the instrument I was leaving or the one I was about to play. Soon I was analyzing what it was (what was emerging) that made the transitional states so attractive to me.

That analysis led to the abstraction of principles for designing more complex instruments that both shared functionality and cross-modulated each other. During the late 60s/early 70s, systems analysis was a prevalent conceptual tool in the world of emerging technology; it fit my studies perfectly, so nested flowcharts with accompanying notations became a way of life for me. To keep a fairly complex business manageable, I'd make flowcharts of all the individual instruments of the set, and then fit them into a larger flowchart, the performance set. Taking the complex flowchart step made it easier to understand what it was that made some systems work so well together musically in their transitional states. (In this paragraph you could just as well substitute the word matrix for the word system.)

During the early 1970s the compositional process of systems design led me to integrate music with other dynamic systems such as air currents, audience movement, circuit design, and flowing light—I began to think of other dynamic systems as higher level modules that could relate to each other in ways similar to the modular functions of electronic music synthesizers, but on higher and more complex levels. At that time I called those compositions "environments"; today they're more likely to be called installations. Intuitively I was modeling the environments on biological systems, and over the course of a few years in the early 1970s I composed a number of multi-day pieces called the Metabiosis Series

Throughout the 1970s and beyond I continued to explore experimentally with the systems approach to composition, while at the same time working to understand physics, psychophysics, cybernetics, metaphysics, biology, and social systems. Early during those explorations it became clear to me that, for the purpose of freeing up the thinking process, it might be helpful to think of all those highly complex systems as multidimensional matrices. When designs really got complex I found that the flowcharts I was making with a systems analysis approach were so full of multileveled feedback loops and nested functions that, as an analytical technique, systems analysis recorded as complex flowcharts was reaching the point of being counterproductive for me.

Today I'll use whatever analytical technique makes sense in the context—one, the other, or both. Flowcharts and notes make good records and good springboards, but for complex systems, flowcharts tend to be too reductive. However, matrix alignment seems a whole lot closer to the way things actually work, so when I brainstorm away from the sources of electronic synthesis (on a walk, in the woods, at the beach, etc.) my thinking leans more toward matrix alignment—it makes it easier for me to visualize relationships. Now, as far as I know, a notational system for aligning multidimensional matrices doesn't yet exist, other than prose, which tends to dance around the intersections. But that's no reason not to use matrix alignment as a conceptual creative/analytical tool—notational systems and flowcharts are great tools for keeping records but matrix alignment makes a far better realtime scope.

One example before I stop. The laser animation/projection system that I designed in 1975 has three different galvo/mirror units, one each for x (horizontal deflection), y (vertical deflection), and z (chopping the laser beam).   Each galvo/mirror has its own particular frequency response curve and predominant resonant frequencies. As a set, those galvo/mirrors can be viewed as a matrix with multiple highly sensitive frequency regions.

Taken together I think of that system as having a personality, as being one example of what I think of as a cyberspirit. To create laser animations with that system, I use an electronic wave system (hardware or software synthesizer) to design instruments that generate audio waveforms/frequencies that go in (visual consonance) and out (visual dissonance) of alignment with the personality quirks (matrix features) of my laser animation/projection system. Simply put, to create laser animations I design a matrix on my synthesizer that is capable of being tuned (being aligned with) on-the-fly to the prominent features of another matrix, my laser animation/projection system—the process can be considered an exercise in matrix alignment.

What I find so attractive about the notion of matrix alignment is that it's very valuable as a metaphor for how living systems communicate with each other. Some of what I was saying in my previous post on matrix alignment dealt with a few of my performance-art communications experiments.

A side note: in a previous post Sergio was expressing his concern for maintaining mystery as a value. On that account I think there's nothing for us to worry about. The history of science is one generation after another debunking the theories and "truths" of the previous generation. What's amusing about it is that the current established generation always behaves as if they're absolutely correct, and that's because western science is really a religion—the current scientist pope and his bishops are infallible, whatever the established generation [Is there a better definition of hubris?]. And that includes the latest love affair with the genome. As the old priests were tying up their genome project along came the next generation screaming that proteins hadn't been properly taken into account ;-)

My personal search is for springboards and portals—motivational keys and glimpses of the infinite—the sphere of the Wizard. Simple needs.

Post Three:

To: Metaesthetics@topica.com
From: Ron Pellegrino <ronpell@mail.microweb.com>
Subject: METALIST: dancing around the intersections
Date: Sat, 2 Mar 2002 22:16:48 -0800

I used the expression "dancing around the intersections" in my recent post with the subject line of "A path to matrix alignment" and it's been bouncing around in my thoughts for days.

The quote from that post:

"Today I'll use whatever analytical technique makes sense in the context—one, the other, or both. Flowcharts and notes make good records and good springboards but for complex systems, flowcharts tend to be too reductive. However, matrix alignment seems much closer to the way things actually work, so when I brainstorm away from the sources of electronic synthesis (on a walk, in the woods, at the beach, etc.) my thinking leans more toward matrix alignment—it makes it easier for me to visualize relationships. Now, as far as I know, a notational system for aligning multidimensional matrices doesn't yet exist other than prose which tends to dance around the intersections. But that's no reason not to use matrix alignment as a conceptual creative/analytical tool—notational systems and flowcharts are great tools for keeping records but matrix alignment makes a far better realtime scope."

First, I don't mean to denigrate prose as a notational system—no surprise that I find it an especially valuable mnemonic when used alone as well as with other collections of symbols. Neither do I mean to devalue the idea of dancing around the intersections. It's actually essential, because that is what breathes life into harmonically based dynamic art—it's what provides the dynamism along with the onsets, the transitions, and the decays. In the compositional designs that I use to generate my laser animations, I move through a series of harmonic relationships that can be reduced to whole number ratios. When the whole number ratios are perfect, a state of stasis sets in, which of course means there is no motion—no motion for very long in dynamic art is not all that interesting. So dancing around the intersections (the whole number ratios) is a crucial aspect of that performance art form—I never do the dance the same way twice even though the sound/light image created by any particular whole number ratio is the same from performance to performance (in a sense it's a constant that, unlike the dance, can actually be notated). What I practice before a performance is the dancing around intersections, the onsets, the transitions, and the decays.

The whole number ratios chosen for sequences (conceptually similar to chord progressions in traditional music) are important compositionally as the substructure of the realtime aspect (the dancing, the transitional states, etc.) of the visual music piece. What needs to be noted is that the whole number ratios are based on the fundamentals of the wavetrains at x, y, and z. Matters are complicated considerably (and what happens in sound/sight gets a whole lot more interesting too) when the wavetrains are complex waveforms with envelopes on their frequencies, amplitudes, and spectra. What that means is that the intersections of the whole number ratios are actually intersections of three evolving multidimensional matrices with additional ratios occurring with the partials that accompany the involved fundamentals. (Harmonic partials have whole number relationships to their fundamentals; inharmonic partials do not.)

Add all of that to the electromechanical galvo/mirrors for x, y, and z (multidimensional matrices as well) and you end up with six multidimensional matrices in search of alignment. Add to those six a small performance group of three—not long ago I worked with another musician and a dancer—and that makes 9 multidimensional matrices, not to mention the instruments the musician was playing, the work of the person lighting the stage, the audience, the context for the event, and...(probably because it's too much like infinite regression, this is where Bob Seiple didn't want to go in one of his recent posts ;-). In that complex there are many levels of alignment—the whole number ratios of the fundamentals, the whole number ratios of the partials of the waveforms, the wavetrains and the galvo/mirrors, the performers, and all of the other matrices in search of alignment, convergence, and right tuning.

What stirred this pot was Mark's recent reference to Pythagoras and Diana's reply to my "A path to matrix alignment" post. Though I didn't refer directly to what Diana said, reading it everyday since she posted it was the big stirring spoon. I'm hoping the above helps to clarify what I mean by the alignment of multidimensional matrices.

13
The Crevices Of Audio Compression

What falls through the cracks in audio compression? The simple unvarnished answer is that what's lost is much of what contributes to musical subtlety. And where does that musical subtlety reside? The answer is in the subtle components of the sound, the first components dumped by compression algorithms because those components have been determined by "scientific testing" to fall below the threshold levels of "normal hearing". The engineer's argument (most people ain't gonna hear that fine stuff anyway) is that for commercial music, it's only necessary to include what's required to make saleable music. Talk about destructive reference points for musical subtlety—"normal hearing" and saleable music.

Removing subtle components from sound reduces the range of feelings, the musical heart and soul, carried by the sound. The process also dampens what's not been removed entirely, particularly in the domain of articulation—onsets, sustain curves, and decays. The spectral components of sound are also adversely affected, and that means that tone quality is compromised. The upshot is that the obvious components of the music are retained whereas the most subtle parts are removed. The main drawback to that approach is that what stops before serving the finer motor parts of hearing will seriously fail at serving the heart and head parts. Nothing much wrong with toe tapping except that, as a reference, it remains one of the lower functions in music.

Compression removes information. What gets removed first is what's most subtle and most dramatic—the softest, the loudest, and the actual sounds of "silence" (actually no such thing) between the notes. What suffers most is the dynamic range—the softest wisps to the wildest whacks. What gets removed is based on our (therefore the engineers making the compression decisions in the design of the algorithms) very limited knowledge of psychoacoustics as it relates to musical values. Who's to determine musical values? The musicians or the audio engineers or both together?

In most cases, both groups are without conceptual and experiential foundations for determining, much less articulating musical values. So audio compression is based on a serious quandary. The subject of musical values is not a significant part of the technical training for music performers or audio technicians, so what we're talking about here is technicians in both music and audio engineering who are trained only in mechanical matters, and not aesthetic matters. They simply haven't been educated in an environment that cultivates the higher values that accompany inspiration in the musical arts. Trained technicians do what they're been trained to do. Their approach is mechanical, not creative. Everyone does their bit but their bits don't necessarily add up to music at its finest. Given the disappointing results that are plain to hear on recordings and reinforced sound in live performances, it seems obvious that neither group knows what they're doing to the music. So who should be trusted with music compression decisions?

Ask around. How many musicians and how many audio engineers have seriously studied the field of the aesthetics of music, the philosophical study of musical values. Not long ago in a conversation with an academic composer, who in California established a thriving university program in music technology and engineering, I was stunned again as he summarily dismissed the value for his program of any subject related to philosophy. He's not the only academic in the music engineering field taking that position. In fact, it's endemic to the field.

If the music to be compressed doesn't have much in the way of subtlety, there's not much to be lost. Music lovers (and that includes the best of the audio engineers) need to understand that the function of compression, as it now stands, is not intended to serve the music; rather it's designed to serve the efficient and economical delivery of music, mostly for commercial purposes. Compression algorithms are designed to reduce file size by discarding audio information that various teams of audio design engineers deemed unnecessary when they configured the algorithms used in both hardware and software.

You've probably heard many of the arguments for dropping sound information—it's above or below the frequency range of ear, it's below the sensitivity threshold of the ear, it's too loud, it's too noisy, the normal person won't notice the difference anyway, etc. With even the least bit of digging those arguments are found to be superficial at best and usually completely specious. For example, the ear is just one part of the hearing system. You also hear with your bones, your body cavities, your organs, and your flesh. Furthermore, you direct your hearing with your intelligence in the form of your attention which is rooted in your experience, expectations, and will. Another example is that resultant tones which are created by the interaction of fundamentals with each other and with their respective spectra may be very subtle phenomena, but therein lies the life of the sound, the life that gets removed because it's carried by information too subtle to make it through the compression algorithm.

If you remove the subtle phenomena, you remove the life embedded in the sound—it's that simple. Another example is concerned with frequencies that are theoretically above the range of hearing but, nevertheless, will still interact (heterodyne) with each other to create resultant tones (difference tones) that fall into the commonly accepted auditory frequency range. When that happens those resultant tones add life and color to the sound—remove them and out goes the life and the color of the sound. The list of examples could go on and on as we examine the musical nature of noise, transients, dynamic levels, phase, and other subtle musical phenomena.

The discussion in the paragraph above is all pure mechanics, but it inflects on metaphysics, an area of thought concerned with where the soul in the sound resides. We won't go into a discussion of soul and sound because it would make most audio mechanics squirm, and although the best musicians understand the connection intuitively, they don't have the conceptual tools to discuss it. But if you're really interested in higher order musical values, don't waste a step when going there, and you would be well served by starting with a book by Hazrat Inayat Khan called *THE MUSIC OF LIFE*.

Any audio recording by its nature is a reduction in the quality and a distortion of the sound that is supposed to serve the music. Each piece of music recording equipment has its own sound signature, a signature that's easy to hear if your hearing system is in good working order. Its unique signature is implied if you can understand how to read and interpret its specification list—upper and lower frequency response limits, response curve (which frequencies it tends emphasize and which it tends to de-emphasize), transient response, types and levels of distortions, and much more including loads of other loss and distortion details that the particular engineering group defining the specifications decided not to include. Add together the colorations (sound signatures) of all those recording devices—microphones, mixers, monitors, etc.—and the result is not what you'd hear if you were in the presence of the living unamplified music where the instruments project the musical information unfettered. Instead, you are treated to canned audio colors only somewhat representative of the music. We are at the point in the history of music where the majority of music consumers (not so long ago it was music lovers) act as though they believe those canned audio colors are the real music, the music just as it should be—a sad state.

What else is there? those music consumers might ask. And they might ask that question because if they go to concerts what they'll most likely hear is music that sounds as though it's been recorded. And that's because it's being amplified and colored by all the usual audio suspects—microphones, mixers, amplifiers, monitors, and the audio engineer at the helm with all his fancy tech on parade. Very few people today hear music that is not colored by an audio amplification system. They have no idea of what they're missing, so of course you can't expect them to care about what they don't know, and that also holds true for most audio engineers who will rarely if ever experience music in its natural acoustic state.

I've been concerned with this problem for many years, but the stimulus for writing this essay was weeks of exploring and testing compression algorithms on my own music that I was preparing to post on my website. After all the time and effort given to finding the best solution, I'm still very unhappy with what happens to my music when it's treated to the compression algorithms targeted at Internet distribution. Yes, I do realize the value of the presentational and demonstrable functions to posting compressed excerpts of my work on my site, but doing so remains a painful exercise in compromise. And that's because compression is actually reflecting my work in a distorted mirror marred by gaps, bumps, and assorted other expulsions.

What bothers me most about posting any of my audio work is that the simple purity of the sound is badly marred by a common digital compression technique. That compression technique involves, at some arbitrary period, doing comparisons of the information fields as they fly by, moment to moment. The tack involves analyzing an audio reference field and then, in the new field, "pointing back" to the reference field to what hasn't changed in the information, and then just documenting what's new and carrying over what "hasn't changed." That technique is designed to save considerable file space (at the cost of musical subtlety). One problem with this tack involves the process of determining just how much change is required to be recognized by the compression algorithm as a change worthy of note. That particular computer technique falls well short of functioning like a human limen, defined as a just noticeable difference, the threshold of a physiological or psychological response. The human acoustic limen is a variable that changes value according to where the event falls in the frequency, amplitude, and spectral ranges, as well as relative to their combinations. That sort of analysis is effortless for good ears and a musical sensibility, but not to be found in compression algorithms, not yet anyway because computer modeling of the human hearing system as it perceives music is still in the early stages.

If the audio information is deemed too subtle by the compression algorithm—good-bye—it falls through the crevice. Another problem is that in the process of creating the fields, the sound is sampled and compared at an arbitrary period, and that results in interruptions that'll mar any music based on continuous sound with subtle variations. The compression algorithm is a machine that adversely affects musical value but don't hold your breath while you're waiting for the audio engineers to own up to it; they and their employers are just waving their hands in a semi-hypnotic fashion and trying to convince you that they're saving you some file space and giving you more for your money. And in a consumer culture, please tell me what's wrong with that? So if you're seriously looking for the answer to "what's wrong with that ?", we're back again to the issue of musical values. Listen closely to music and compare the real spirit food with the canned stuff. Be experimental. Go to acoustic concerts. Your ears will be pleased with the nuanced input, and so will your brain.

14
Why Care About Sonification?

What follows is a response to questions about important applications of sonification (the use of non-speech sound for modeling, exploring, and conveying information in the arts and science). The questions were posed in a message over the ICAD (International Community for Auditory Display) mailing list from David H. Jameson, Manager, Computer Music Center, IBM Research Division. My first reaction to his message was one of irritation because I tend to chafe at the way some people use mailing lists to get subscribers to do their thinking for them. But the question of "why the world should care about sonification" kept invading my mind-space for days so I gave in to the irritant and organized my thoughts on the matter and posted it to the list. Jameson's post to the ICAD list is found at the end of my response.

Why the world should care about sonification.

To: David Jameson <dhj@watson.ibm.com>, icad@santafe.edu
From: Ron Pellegrino <ronpell@microweb.com>?
Subject: RE: What's a compelling example of sonification?
Date: 9/15/98

At the root level, the "killer" apps for sonification are learning and playing, what most creative people would consider fundamental reasons for being. Certain segments of the education and entertainment industries target the learning and playing processes, so for those particular segments sonification must be considered a critical component of their work. Any person or institution involved in emerging sonification technology that gets in step with those industrial segments stands to gain in terms of both finances and well-being.

The flip side of sonification is visualization. Smell, taste, and touch aside, people perceive and remember many natural events from combinations of their unique auditory and visual emanations. Intuitively the human sensory system records experiences of auditory/visual events as both individualized and integrated memory fields. Those events can be recalled either as auditory or as visual memories with the emphasis placed on one or the other. Or they can be recalled as integrated auditory/visual memory fields which will have greater depth, complexity, and meaning than either field alone. The integration of sonification and visualization creates a lifelike experience that makes learning faster, richer, and deeper, and makes playing more exciting and more aesthetically rewarding.

The reason sonification has become an issue is because we're working with a tool (the digital computer) that evolved along the lines of a calculator or business machine—the BM in

IBM. Given that the computer is based on numbers (abstractions) and not commonly shared human experiences, we find ourselves in the throes of trying to turn numbers into semblances of life (not so different from turning lead into gold, so a little alchemy is in order) and life into numbers (so they can begin to represent commonly shared human experiences). For decades leading up to the 1990s, computer science mostly insisted that practitioners wear digital blinders to avoid analog seduction (leaving the good times for sound and light artists); so hybrid processes such as analog/digital/analog for sonification were slow to enter the mainstream which seemed more interested in generating, counting and distributing money. Although those hybrid processes found the way to the mainstream in the late 1990s, few people have either the experiential or theoretical background to make good use of them, but that seems about to change. [The virtual reality bubble in the 1990s involved an impressive collection of creative minds promoting hybrid processes, but the unrealized commercial hype was the prick that burst that bubble.]

Although it's still in the early developmental stages, another "killer" app for sonification (and visualization) is the stimulation its study provides for exploring psychophysics including psychoacoustics and psychooptics. Hubris notwithstanding, for those with college educations the current intellectual grasp of all things hearing and seeing barely registers on the meter. It's just during the past few decades that we've had the mechanical and conceptual tools to explore perception in measured and comparative ways. During that time the growing emphasis on computer modeling of natural phenomena has shaped programs at some of our top academic and government research centers. Nevertheless, it's still been a relatively slow go because institutional recognition and support of such "blue sky" research into psycho-matters has been confined to just a few places, leaving much of the work to be done by the self-motivated without much institutional support. Though still relatively incipient, this particular app could eventually be the most important culturally. Imagine what a cultural difference it would make if we had a K-12 educational system designed around the how, what, why, and care and feeding of the senses instead of just preparing our children to be good consumers and industrial cogs.

What I'm saying here is not just a theoretical rant. My own life took a new tack in 1967 when I discovered for myself the value of the integrated sonification/visualization approach; that's when I decided to take on learning the Moog Synthesizer as part of my Ph.D. dissertation project. I was a classically educated multi-instrumentalist and composer with little experience in physics and electronics, but when I heard and saw the synthesizer for the first time, I recognized that it was the composer's instrument of the future so I decided to take it on as a project. Other than a few of Moog's very sketchy spec sheets, there was absolutely no instructional material available for the music synthesizer in 1967. So I spent nine months with a decent stereo sound system and a dual trace oscilloscope exploring the ins and outs of all the wave train generation and modification functions of all the modules on the Moog; the log of what I learned from that process became one-third of my dissertation project as well as the basic text for the Moog Synthesizer wherever it was found.

For me and most other composers sonification had always been the normal state of affairs; what was different from 1967 onwards was that I started integrating sonification with visualization in the learning, and eventually the composing and teaching processes. Because the academic world of the 70s and 80s, even up into the early 90s, was populated by legions of Luddites dressed like administrators, faculty, and students, the emerging technology in the arts facilities that I organized at various universities for teaching and production tended to be seed-islands in an ocean of doubts. During the past three decades my teaching/research spaces and public presentations have included the full range of affordable emerging technology for sonification/visualization including analog, digital and hybrid synthesizers, general and specialized computers with special software and peripherals, laser deflector/projectors, audio and video recording and playback gear, audio and visual translation and conversion equipment, and all manner of analytical and measurement gear. I personally have shown my work to many thousands of people and I know that numerous other composers have been working along similar lines, so I suspect we must be on the verge of a critical mass that will lead to a general awareness and acceptance of the validity of sonification/visualization in learning and playing.

The latest upwelling in multimedia [during the 1990s] is partly an attempt to harness for commercial purposes the work that's been done in the past few decades in the sonification/visualization fields. Not much of value has come out of this recent multimedia wave because most of those involved are barely conversant with the fundamental issues of sonification/visualization, issues which are subjects of the study of psychophysics. At best, their work tends to be rooted in Saturday morning animated cartoons rather than a fundamentally serious study of psychophysics; at worst, their work is rootless and mindless, just as following any other fad might be.

Anyone who doesn't care about sonification risks missing out on one of the next major leaps in computer technology—the humanization of the computer and computer experiences. For the mainstream, working on sonification, visualization, and other sensory conversions and translations should provide the irritants and the inspiration to help spring the computer out of the mechanical world into the biological world. Dynamical artists working in sound and light have been learning to play on that field for decades. It's time now for the mainstream.

Below is the email that triggered this essay on sonification:

>Date: Thu, 10 Sep 1998
>To: icad@santafe.edu, sound@acm.org, auditory@vm1.mcgill.ca
>From: David Jameson <dhj@watson.ibm.com>
>Subject: What's a compelling example of sonification?

>Suppose you were a keynote speaker at the next COMDEX exhibition. Your job
>is to explain to the audience why the world should care about sonification.
>What would you tell them? What do you think are the potential "killer" apps
>that takes sonification out of the niche world into the mainstream?
>There are some obvious examples for particular communities (e.g. screen
>readers for the visually disabled, perhaps the use of sound in games for

>informational purposes) but I'm wondering what applications of sonification
>might make a really significant percentage of people take notice and think
>"I gotta have this" or even "hmmm, I'm going to buy a computer so I can
>have this", specifically because of the sonification.

>I look forward to your thoughts,

>Cheers,

>David Jameson

>_____
>Dr. David H. Jameson
>Manager, Computer Music Center
>IBM Research Division
>Route 134 & Taconic State Parkway
>Yorktown Heights, NY 10598

THREE

Visual Music

15
Visual Music Flavors

Visual Music is an integrated multimedia approach to music based on the principle that there are both natural visual manifestations and invented visual representations of all sonic musical elements, structures, and processes. Visual music forms emerge from the integration of the physics, psychophysics, and metaphysics of sound, light, form, and movement as well as the marriage of current and emerging art technology with the long rich tradition of the art of performance. Flavors of visual music are the outcome of the various approaches to realizing this principle according to various applications in performance art, entertainment, visual art, and education.

The popularization and accessibility of multimedia tools are two of a number of forces driving the growing interest in visual music and the desire by artists, scientists, and educators of all stripes and ranks to be associated with the idea of visual music. Visual music is just one facet of many in the ongoing visualization revolution in education, communications, the sciences, and the arts. Visualization tools such as the current crop of sound and image generators and recorders, specialized AV microcomputers, test equipment, and relatively inexpensive yet powerful software for doing high quality multimedia are commonplace today in homes, artist studios, science laboratories, business places, and classrooms. Add to that technology mix the genre called "creativity" software (algorithms and generative systems that make it relatively easy for the any user to produce the illusion of a work of art) and a genuinely joyful creative attitude that seems to be picking up steam in many segments of society, and the upshot is that conditions are ripe for a bountiful visual music harvest.

Once you begin to examine what people are calling visual music, it becomes abundantly clear from the rich variety of approaches that there must be a corresponding variety of notions of what people believe belongs in the sphere of music. The following visual music flavors grow out of those notions.

Visual Music Flavors

1. Literal visualizations of music are generated directly from channelized musical wavetrains.

2. Imagery and music emerge from one and the same algorithmic process.

3. Visualization systems are mapped to some of the symbols used in traditional music scores.

4. Scrolling scores in software MIDI sequencers bring the look of the traditional piano roll to the digital age.

5. Software for the creation, animation, and sequencing of graphics that spins out musical gestures is modeled on the principles of MIDI sequencers.

6. Interpretive visualizations emerge from dance and theater traditions that undoubtedly extend back to the dawn of human religious and celebratory rituals.

7. Object oriented programming environments are endowed with flowcharting procedures that represent instruments or orchestras that can virtually play themselves or be performed by artists.

8. Appropriately dramatic, humorous, or lyrical music closely synchronized with natural or invented moving imagery is now a mainstay of the popular media scene especially in advertising, but also in commercial television and films.

9. Musical materials and/or gestures are mapped to imagery to create visual instruments that are meant to be played by a variety of input devices.

10. Using their shallow understanding of the collaborative philosophies of John Cage and Merce Cunningham as an argument for just about anything goes, some music visualizers combine photos or paintings or drawings or the outputs of algorithmic/generative animation systems with live or recorded music and rely entirely on coincidence and the natural predisposition of the minds of the audience/spectators to create implicit order out of exactly or nearly simultaneous sensory events.

11. Landing somewhat closer to the Cage/Cunningham target are two related approaches; the first is based on simultaneous realtime composition by sound, image, and body movement collaborators; the second involves performances by an individual creating music with self-precomposed imagery or creating realtime imagery with self-precomposed music.

12. Some performing musicians are so at one with their music that they move their bodies in ways that articulate every nuance of the music they're creating, as well as articulating the thought process that lead to the music they're creating. Not so long ago I was in an audience that was treated by Steve Williams, the drummer with The Shirley Horn Trio, to a transcendental evening of visual music drumming; his movements were one with the sounds he created. Choreographers and dancers would do well to study the drama and lyricism of the organic movement of musicians like Steve Williams. No posturing. No affectations. No waste. All one—movement and music.

13. Audio software manufacturers rely heavily on analytical routines to visualize audio recording, editing, processing, and mixing. Many of their software programs are so highly evolved that they make excellent resources for multi-modal learning and teaching of music fundamentals based on the physical nature of sound, human perception of sound, how music instruments work, auditorium acoustics, and music recording and playback systems.

14. Any good book, article, film, video, or DVD on the science of sound should be packed with charts, diagrams, and illustrations that serve to clarify the basic principles that connect music with the fields of physics, psychology, physiology, mathematics, speech, engineering, audiology, architecture, and other related fields.

15. Sonification of visual forms and natural events is a sphere of activity that intersects with music visualization, enough so to be consider a candidate for another visual music flavor even though a flip is required. Sonifying or translating into music natural dynamical systems such as weather, ocean currents, planetary or celestial movement, solar storms, and the like has gained currency and momentum since its beginnings in the early 1970s.

16. Rude and crude. The use of sound and light forms that use levels, rhythms, and effects that are psychophysically painful and possibly injurious. Commonly the perpetrators of this flavor, for legal reasons, include a disclaimer. Be forewarned; carry earplugs and be prepared to close your eyes. Despite those precautions, high intensity percussive events or strobe light effects at just the right (wrong!) tempo (pulse rate) can negatively affect the heart and nervous system; and loud, low sound near the sub-audio threshold can do the same sort of damage to your digestive system. At one of the finest concert venues in Berkeley, CA I was forced to inform the audio tech who was working the board that if he insisted on overdriving the low frequencies and my stomach decided to rebel, it's output would be over his board. He wisely and kindly backed off the low frequencies and all ended well.

As the internet grew exponentially during the 1990s I came across increasing numbers of artists who wanted their work to be associated with the notion of visual music. It was during that time that I gradually became ever more uneasy with the "flavor" metaphor as descriptive of the various approaches taken to visual music. Just imagine it's possible that ice cream could be flavored with garlic, artichoke, potato, basil, or even unmentionables and still be considered an ice cream treat by some folks with strange inclinations; but common sense says that those incongruent flavors seriously digress from the notion of the sweet desert that comes to most minds when the object is said to be ice cream. Similarly the essence of visual music grows out of the principle stated above—**there are both natural visual manifestations and invented visual representations of all sonic musical elements, structures, and processes**—and the more congruent the flavors are with that notion, the closer the works are to the core of what's meant by the expression, visual music. Contrary to the desires of so many who want to be associated with the field of visual music because it has a certain cachet in the avant-garde, there's far more to the field than simply combining any sound with any dynamic imagery willy-nilly. To put it precisely, to be included in the visual music field, a work's dynamic imagery should be variously informed by the music, integrated with the music, embody the music, and/or grow out of the music.

16
Graphic Scores

During the 1960s and early 1970s many composers in the experimental music movement placed very strong emphasis on graphic scores for music. Unlike traditional music scores, which are in fact also exceedingly graphic in their own very precise way, the graphic scores of the experimentalists rarely required the specificity of exact pitches, durations, or any other musical elements. Instead they created their own symbolic notation that visually or graphically suggested time-based gestures, frequency curves, articulation regimes, and whatever else they deemed appropriate for the context they were creating. In effect, graphic scores are symbolic invitations to performing musicians to participate in the compositional process.

Unquestionably my visual music work has roots in that graphic tradition of the experimental music movement of the 1960s. As a young composer and academic during that period, I found myself drawn to the interpretive freedom that graphic scores encouraged as creative exercises. Because the process was by its nature always challenging and edifying, I organized student and faculty groups of the more adventurous spirits at The Ohio State University and Oberlin College to collaborate on interpreting a broad range of such scores. That included working with the scores of well-known composers such as John Cage to the scores of students and colleagues on and off the campuses. One of my favorite sources of graphic scores was a collection of computer printouts by the composer Herbert Brün. What I found especially intriguing about Brün's work was that he experimented with composing computer algorithms that generated both desirable graphic printouts (visual music) and computer generated music from one and the same algorithm. Although in the literary expositions of his work he did not emphasize the point, his work was definitely an exploration of the common ground for the eye and the ear.

One of the few misgivings I have about the graphic scores from that period was that they are themselves mostly static. Of course you could make the same statement about traditional scores; they sit very still on the page expecting that the performer start reading from the beginning at the upper left corner, continue reading the notation left to right, continue with the successive staves top to bottom, go on to the next page and repeat the process until you reach the end of the piece. What I enjoyed about Brün's algorithmic scores was that the performers were free to decide collectively how to move through the imagery. All well and good, but the audience still couldn't see the score; they were out of the loop.

In my own graphic scores (film, video, and laser animations) I experimented with ways to bring the audience into the creative loop both as observers and as critics and virtual players (perhaps thinking, "Oh, wasn't that clever!" or "I would have done it this way rather than their way"). To function best as a dynamic graphic score, the imagery must be writ large, projected so both performers and audience can view the unfolding; thus, large projections were part of my plan from the beginning. Projecting the imagery helps to focus audience attention on the process and stimulates their imaginations as well. This contributes to an improved performance environment because performers always do better work when they sense that the audience is somehow engaged in the process.

Beginning in the early 1970s I put my synthesizer driven oscillographic films to work as dynamic graphic scores. While I was still working with film, I started researching the viability of video as a visual music medium. My earliest research was done at the National Center for Experiments in Television, located at the time in San Francisco at KQED, part of the Public Television Network; the NCET facility was supported by the Rockefeller Foundation and my work was supported by Oberlin College and the National Endowment for the Humanities. A few years later in 1974 I collaborated with a group of self-supported projected light artists (many worked the West Coast rock light shows of the 1960s) at Project Artaud, an art community centered in the warehouse district of San Francisco in an area that eventually became known as Multimedia Gulch in the 1990s. In both cases those were rare opportunities because we had access to one-of-a-kind video synthesizers, the earliest video projectors and recorders, and spacious and well-equipped research and performance spaces. Some of our collaborations were programmed on Real* Electric Symphony performances at galleries, concert spaces, and the art and science museums in the San Francisco Bay Area.

Early in 1975 when I began to explore synthesizer driven laser animations as dynamic graphic scores, I realized that it was the medium that best met my needs at the time for composition and performance. Unlike film and video, it is its own projection medium and it doesn't involve costs related to a studio, film stock or tape, recorders, special editing gear, slow and difficult-to-control-quality services, or storage. I never returned to filmmaking and didn't pick up the video thread again until 1983 when I began connecting the NTSC output, of first an Apple IIe and then other computers, to video monitors and projectors.

I also began collecting animation software that I could perform in realtime, the way I work with the laser animation system. The computer outputs easily to video so, heartfelt thanks to all the great animation software creators, the computer quickly became the video synthesizer for the masses, as it is now. What's thrown away as screen savers today would have made light artists in the 1960s and 70s salivate.

It's worth noting that the history sketched in the previous paragraphs became the production basis for the four DVDs included in the *Emergent Music and Visual Music* package. Rather than a film camera, I used a video camera to capture laser animations. Rather than recording the imagery to film stock, it was recorded first onto analog videotape and then converted to digital data. Rather than editing the dynamic graphic segments on a Steenbeck film editing machine, I used inexpensive computer software for video editing. Rather than using rare, expensive, and bulky video synthesizers, I used affordable computer animation software that generated imagery that might never leave the digital domain unless you play the DVDs on a video monitor rather than a computer. A few of us still remember when all of these games were little more than smoke dreams.

17
Playing Free Of The Video Box

What follows is what I wrote in response to some remarks by Stephen Malinowski [a leading music visualizer who excels in both vision and execution] in reference to issues that surfaced in the course of our participation in a day-long gathering of music visualizers at Dennis Keefe's video facility in Alameda, California on July 11, 1999. My first response addresses the following issues:

- Playing free of the video box
- My conceptual models for laser imagery
- Visual music holy grail
- What you see is what you hear and what you hear is what you see
- I'm not a fan of any current recording medium
- Dynamic structures and feelings

The follow-up response addresses these additional issues:

- Memory of art experience
- The function of philosophy

To: Stephen Malinowski <smalin@well.com>, bindu@slip.net, bmr@best.com, flc2@po.cwru.edu, hoekman@apple.com, cuba@well.com, spot@transmeta.com, greg@imaja.com, aschloss@finearts.uvic.ca, david@tristram.com
From: ronpell@microweb.com
Subject: feedback loop?
Date: 7/18/99

Hi Folks:

I figured the group would be interested in my response to Stephen's remarks directed to me.

Malinowski - Ron, when you first showed me your laser art in your home studio, I asked about videotape, and you said something which I've since recalled as "never" (I'm not known for my memory, though). I was so happy to see you'd changed your stance a little on this. It's true that the videotape is a pale reproduction of the purity, intensity, and perfection of the original, but so what? An audio CD is likewise a pale reproduction of a live performance. But with both, the reproduction is still a viable thing, and I thought they looked very good. My only disappointment was that you didn't show the piece which has the two (or was it three) sine (or were they?) tones that slide around continuously. You know the one I mean, don't you? If you EVER, EVER, EVER get that piece on videotape, could I PLEASE, PLEASE, PLEASE have a copy? When you were talking, I wrote down the phrase "dynamic structures and feelings," with the plan of talking to you about it. But I've already forgotten the context. If you remember, could you remind me so I can pick up the thread? (I'm enjoying the new stuff on your website, BTW.)

Pellegrino - What I love about music driven laser animation is that it plays free of the video box or any other display limitations unless you choose to have them; and it does it with a light quality that is inimitable. With video, computer animation, and film (I made a series of five music synthesizer generated visual music films in the early 70s that I used in my shows for a decade as dynamic graphic scores that I taught musicians to realize or sonify), I always feel awfully restricted by the set window—the size, the aspect ratio, the light quality—and, especially with video, the resolution. When I work with those media, one of my favorite games is to suggest the space beyond the confines by having visual objects move in and out the space beyond the edges of the window, and by using imagery that breathes at the edges of the confines in such a way that when it expands and contracts, parts of it move out into the space beyond and then back to the inside again.

The solution for my performance-multimedia work includes using a large video projection screen (at least 12' x 9') flanked by multiple (four or more) video monitors of at least 27" and setting up my performance work station in the pit or on the floor just below the stage, so the audience can also see me working with the video camera, the computer digitizing and processing system, and the three small video monitors that I use to make editing decisions on-the-fly. Plus when I work with those media I always include live performers of all persuasions. The upshot is that the audience can choose what to attend to and when to attend to it. The projection screen, the monitors, the process unfolding at my workstation, the musicians, the dancers, the realtime theater lighting action, and roving video camera people all function as visual variables. So for my work, video and computer animations become modules in a large complex system that definitely operates beyond the confines of any boxed system such as video or film.

One of my goals in composing laser imagery is to give it a sense of being alive and freeing it from as many physical limitations as possible. My conceptual models for the laser imagery are life forms and processes, especially those that might resonate with the people in the audience. Those life forms and processes do not exist in low resolution boxes with fixed aspect ratios. At best, our standard visual displays always strike me as being peep shows on the processes that lie behind the creation of the imagery. In contrast, the music is out there in multidimensional acoustic space bouncing and curving and mixing and having a great free time of it until it fades beyond our perceptual capabilities and escapes to become part of life's background. And, of course, live performers play their games in their own multidimensional spaces. Laser animations fit well in that world.

The raw video tape I showed of laser imagery and sound emerging from the same synthesized wavetrains (in effect, the imagery and sound were flip sides of a set of coins (composed/performed stereo wavetrains)) was composed for a number of purposes including self-education (meditation) and compositional studies. I titled the tape Visual Music Meditations because it's part of the process that I'm using to educate myself on the various paths leading to the visual music holy grail (from my perspective) which is visual music work that demonstrates the principle of "what you see is what you hear and what you hear is what you see"—different facets of the same fundamental yet complex dynamical process (the wavetrains). I'm also composing pieces that use the material on that tape as the conductor of the MIDI orchestras I love designing. For that purpose I'm using a MIDI facility which is completely integrated with the video digitizing/processing/mixing wing of one of my studios.

Glasssongs, the laser piece that Stephen is referring to, is actually one of my earliest attempts in the realm of "what you see is what you hear and what you hear is what you see." It was composed in 1983 on an Apple IIe running an alphaSyntauri, the first affordable stereo digital audio synthesizer, an instrument that predated MIDI, but conceptually incorporated much of what we now know as MIDI. For that piece I designed an orchestra modeled on a huge glass harmonica which is why Stephen refers to it as "the piece which has the two (or was it three) sine (or were they?) tones that slide around continuously." I've been programming that piece in concerts since it was composed in 1983 and it still is an audience favorite. A few years ago when I started the music driven laser animation recording project, "Glasssongs" was at the very top of my recording list. Conceived to be free, it refused to be forced into a box—so, sorry Stephen, no video recording. Far better that it exists in an exalted form in Stephen's memory than in a pale distorted form on a videotape. **[The animated laser imagery for Pythagoras & Pellegrino In Petaluma was designed specifically for video recording. The imagery was projected onto a screen, picked up by a video camera, and split out to video and audio monitors as well as to a recording deck. I looked only at the video monitors to make those pieces. Most of the generating systems were my designs that I studied and tweaked previously for decades. From my collection I only used those that agreed with the notion of video confinement.]**

In a nutshell what I'm saying is that I'm not a fan of any current recording medium although I admit to using them because they're so handy and helpful in many ways. Stephen says "It's true that the videotape is a pale reproduction of the purity, intensity, and perfection of the original, but so what?" The answer to Stephen's "so what?" is that I personally prefer the depth, richness, and intensity of the actual primary experience to the secondary "pale reproduction" of that event. One can choose to make the effort to attend live events. The reward is the same reward that accompanies attending anything that's living—it's special because it's here and then quickly gone, a one time affair. It's the only way to make contact with the sublime, and the experience seems to create the appetite for feeling that way again. With anything that's canned, repeated experiences of it tend to be ever duller—neural scientists call the process habituation

On average, in search of inspiration, I attend over 50 live performances in the arts annually [easy to do in the San Francisco Bay Area] and I seldom use recorded media except as modules to be mixed with realtime events in my performances. There's something extra special about the ephemeral nature of the primary experience when compared to the mechanical and determinate nature of the same event recorded. What I've just said should help to explain why my presentation won't be included on the videotape record of the gathering's presentations. I asked that it not be recorded because my business policy since the late

1970s has been to turn down all requests to present my work in any recorded form. That decision is equal parts quality control and business strategy. Although I've lost a few friends and colleagues along the way since that decision, my "no recording policy" has served the paid live presentation aspect of my work very well; plus when I'm there in the flesh I know my work will get the best possible presentation given the overall conditions. [So the DVDs included in this project are a radical departure from my previous approach to the business end of the game.]

I often use the expression "dynamic structures and feelings" in reference to *FEELING AND FORM*, Susanne K. Langer's classic book on the theory of art, a book I studied as a doctoral student in a philosophy seminar at the University of Wisconsin. That study, plus undergraduate work focusing on her earlier book, *PHILOSOPHY IN A NEW KEY*, helped me clarify and articulate what I'd known intuitively since my early days in music. In her book she makes a beautiful case for the power of dynamical art structures to influence human feeling by way of morphological resonances. It boils down to the idea that the microstructural and macrostructural unfolding of time-based art (music, film, video, dance, etc.) evokes human feelings that have similar temporal structures. Any lover of dynamic art understands that notion intuitively when they say they've been moved by an art experience. Of course the idea of morphological resonances, like any good fundamental principle, goes beyond the bounds of dynamic art and applies across the spectrum of life.

Ron Pellegrino

Follow-up Exchange to Playing Free of the Video Box

To: Stephen Malinowski <smalin@well.com>
From: Ron Pellegrino <ronpell@microweb.com>
Subject: Re: feedback loop?
Cc: bindu@slip.net, bmr@best.com, flc2@po.cwru.edu, hoekman@apple.com, cuba@well.com, spot@transmeta.com, greg@imaja.com, aschloss@finearts.uvic.ca, david@tristram.com
Date: 8/2/99

Malinowski - Well, I can hardly take exception to your "quality control" justification for not circulating your work on videotape; video will never capture the intensity and purity of a laser light. (Nor am I any more a fan of any current recording medium than you are.) And while I think you may be mistaken about the business sense of preventing your work from circulating in pale reproductions (for a counterexample, consider the Grateful Dead's policy about pirate tapes of their shows), it's certainly possible you're right and I'm wrong (and since your business has been what I would call a success, it's hard for me to criticize your policy). However, when you say "Far better that it exists in Stephen's memory than in a pale distorted form on a videotape," you can't possibly be taking into account how pale and distorted my memory is!

Pellegrino - I offer my views only as my views—not as the ultimate truth or a path for anyone else to follow. The Grateful Dead and I live in very different worlds; I definitely wouldn't want any part of theirs and they probably wouldn't care much for mine either. I do a lot of experimentation to find what works best for me and when that stops working, I'm always ready to start experimenting again.

I don't expect anyone, regardless of the quality of their memory, to hold all the details of my work in their memory. But when anyone of your caliber says "If you EVER, EVER, EVER get that piece on videotape, could I PLEASE, PLEASE, PLEASE have a copy?" I figure that the ideas and feelings in my piece left the desired impact and that's what I'd like people to remember, the impact.

Malinowski - I'm reading Susanne Langer's _Feeling and Form_ now; thanks for the pointer. It doesn't hold up very well as philosophy (IMHO, though I haven't read it all yet, nor have I read _Philosophy in a New Key_ which she says is necessary preparation), but it has lots of good ideas nonetheless, and like you said, it puts words on things that musicians know intuitively. Although it doesn't say anything one way or another about her, she seems to have a musician's knowledge of music (e.g. the book contains musical scores, so I presume she can read music), which takes her a great ways; too bad, though, that she wasn't also a composer; her ideas about musical expression would have been better if she'd had more direct knowledge of what a composer actually does, and why.

Best,

S.

Pellegrino - I'm not certain what you mean when you say that "It doesn't hold up very well as philosophy." Normally the function of philosophy is to investigate truths and principles, and when the branch of philosophy is aesthetics, the truths and principles are anything but hard and fast. What I like about Langer's thinking is that it goes well beyond what people normally think of as music and includes the investigation of principles that work in all the time-based, dynamic arts. I think that "if she'd had more direct knowledge of what a composer actually does, and why" she'd only know what she was thinking as a composer. It seems to me that what all composers do and why they do it are completely personal matters that are different from composer to composer.

Regards,

Ron

18
The Hewlett-Packard Session

The Real* Electric Symphony was an idea for a performance group I realized beginning in 1975. The realization morphed from event to event depending upon specific event variables including purpose, location, setting, and available resources such as funding, gear, and who was game to play. The different forms The Real* Electric Symphony events took included numerous public performances in the San Francisco Bay Area at venues such as the Berkeley Museum of Art, UC-Berkeley Lawrence Hall of Science, The Exploratorium and Old First Church in San Francisco, other Bay Area universities, cultural centers, art galleries, and even the streets. It extended to public performances on international tours of presentation spaces in South America and Europe sponsored by the US State Department.

The Hewlett-Packard session was characteristic of another one of the forms The Real* Electric Symphony assumed—extended gatherings of performance artists to engage in the audio and/or video recording of a realtime compositional process born of a conversational approach to creating performance art, an approach that encouraged the participants to bring to bear whatever they wanted to offer of their history and insight into the moment. These gatherings could go on all day and all night and into the wee hours of morning, or for days on end, or in the case of the Hewlett-Packard session, all day long and well into the evening.

The Hewlett-Packard session took shape in early 1984 through the good graces of Diane Kitchell, a Santa Rosa graphic artist involved with video art. I met Diane through Ylem, an art and technology community that met often in San Francisco at the Exploratorium and other art and science spaces. Diane, who was familiar with my work in the electronic arts, suggested that I might be interested in meeting some HP artist/engineers also involved in integrating electronic music and the dynamic visual arts. We met and spent an evening in one of my Petaluma studios, during which I showed some of my oscillographic films and music-generated laser animations; it didn't take very long before we set up a gathering for play and recording purposes at the Hewlett-Packard campus in Santa Rosa.

That session took place in a very large space that easily accommodated all the gear and all the North Bay players who were flowing in and out of the scene all day long. The visual gear included a huge video projector and screen that everyone could easily see as well as multiple video monitors scattered among the players. All the large video screens showed the same visual material, the material that was output from an experimental video synthesizer created by Paul Gleaves, an HP engineer at that time who eventually went to work with Grass Valley on NASA projects. Given that this happened in 1984, it might not be too surprising that Paul's video synthesizer was built around a very extended Apple IIe. His synthesizer was designed to generate its own imagery as well as to accept external video inputs and external audio as control inputs.

For this recording session the external video input to Paul's synthesizer was the output of a video camera that Diane pointed at a glass beaded screen, which was reflecting the laser animations I was generating with my Synthi AKS. Paul processed and mixed my laser animations with what he was generating directly on his video synthesizer. Since everyone could see all the screens simultaneously, the evolution of the combined imagery was similar to what you might expect from a couple (more in our case) of people dancing together.

In the same space at the same time, the musicians, on various instruments including keyboard synthesizers and electric guitars, assumed their roles in a conversational mix made audible to all through a great speaker system. The electronic sound they created could also be used as a control input to Paul's video synthesizer and applied to various video variables, so at times the music can be seen influencing image size, color, and location as well as actually triggering video image generation. Thus, everyone could simultaneously see and hear everything that was happening so the session was based on the cross influences of the imagery and music. Periodically the free play would stop and we would somehow agree that what we had just been exploring was worth recording. Then we switched on the video recorder which was also recording the audio mix. For the final step, the recording, we shaped in a more refined way the sound and light we had just been exploring.

Following that very simple path, we spent over nine hours moving, seemingly with the greatest of ease, from one visual music complex to another with no individual in charge. It's always a very special time when performance personnel are adept at being harmonious, and that was one of those times. Somehow harmony was maintained even as guests arrived and departed and musicians did the same forming slightly different music groups as the session unfolded. The mainstays of the music group were HP artist/engineers Jim Smith, Dan Powers, and Michael Kohl, but word of the session was out and around and other North Bay musicians came to play too. I'm writing this description in 2008, over 24 years after the event, but I remember it as if it happened yesterday. That was an event that had staying power.

Among the titles of pieces found on DVD Volumes 1 and 2, you will find the abbreviation SR HP; that abbreviation indicates that the material is drawn from the recording session at the Santa Rosa Hewlett-Packard campus. The Flights (another word in the titles) are various group compositional flights of fancy, another way of referring to the realtime compositional process. During that recording session we took 8 clearly defined flights. Included on the DVDs are all 8 flights titled SR HP Flight 1 through 8.

19
Suggestions For Using The Visual Music Studies

1. **As Dynamic Graphic Scores with or without the recorded audio:** Stimulate the imaginations and creative urges of performers by asking them to analyze and interpret the imagery as notational systems suggestive of traditional compositional variables such as motives, phrases, themes, transitions, developments, and larger structural elements involving repetition, extension, variation, contrast, and surprise. Jazzers and those with experimental tendencies might find this easier initially, but all performers should benefit from the exercise and the attempt. Programming the results of your explorations is a good way to provide incentive for the performers and inspiration for those in the audience who might be open to expressive vehicles that encourage freedom in an art form, especially an art form that promotes the benefits of exploring experimental social systems.

2. **As Performance Pieces:** Offer your community something out of the ordinary. Put the pieces on a concert and use the accompanying descriptions as program notes. All that's required is an appropriate presentational space, a DVD player, a good video playback system, and a good audio playback system. For an uninitiated general audience one piece may be enough, because too much new information for eyes and ears tends to overwhelm even those with the best intentions. More sophisticated audiences probably will be able to handle more pieces because, with their more extensive experience, the information should be less novel and taxing to them.

3. **As Compositional Material:** Build new pieces by appropriating material from the Studies. Experiment with various sequences and mixes. Challenge the imaginations of fellow collaborators or competitors by restricting all of their efforts to just a single study or a limited number of them.

4. **As resources for refining the connections between your hearing and seeing:** With the laser animations take note of the one-to-one correspondences of the sound and the imagery. Alternate letting your ears lead, then letting your eyes lead; this is an exercise that can sharpen and increase the flexibility of both your hearing and your seeing. On successive days return to the same study and notice how much more you both hear and see.

5. **As an approach to intensifying the life of your perceptions and making them far richer:** Simply carry the exercise of observing sound/light connections over to your everyday life. For example, a few days before writing this section I went to a duet concert by an experimental jazz guitarist and a drummer. Appreciating the somewhat esoteric music the jazzers were making had to be a stretch for anyone, but even more so for the beautiful little 7 or 8 year old girl in a pink dress who was there in full view with her father on the side of

the stage; they were forced to sit there because the hall was packed and they walked in just before the music started. Her father dampened her urge to talk to him during the performances but let her express herself in an uninhibited way to the music as it was created by the jazzers, mostly on-the-fly.

I'll never forget the experience of watching that child respond to very demanding music as if she were a live nerve end. She was in a state of nonstop movement, much of which was tightly integrated with the music. Because she was a child, her concentration would occasionally wane, but after a brief disconnect she would jump back into the music sometimes literally, dancing in the air as her legs were just hanging over the front of the chair. The expressions on her face were as active and revealing as the movements of the rest of her body.

For as long as I can remember I've been a great lover of dance in all its forms; I would rank that little girl's musical movements among the greatest of my dance viewing experiences. There are many others in that category, but most of them do **not** involve the professional work of choreographers and dancers whose movements tend to be more acted than authentic. The professionals may be more technically accomplished as performers but they're seldom as moving emotionally as the uninhibited natural movement of that little girl in the pink dress—she was the genuine article. Did I mentioned that her movement was sprinkled with hugs and a kiss or two for her dad?

6. **As vehicles for learning to tune all the video and audio variables on your DVD playback system**: If I were playing the DVDs for you, I'd adjust those variables until the sound and light results were as close as possible to the original experiences, experiences I've had for decades but most likely relatively unknown or at least somewhat new to you. So the point is for you to experiment with tuning the video and audio variables so what you hear and see works best for you at whatever level of experience you may have in the visual music field. You can expect a good return on the efforts given to those tuning experiments. Don't be bashful about playing with the DVD controls.

For any of us, getting close to the original experience is as good as it's going to get. At one time or another you may find the audio too raw; if that happens, adjust the audio level to suit your situation remembering that you'll hear deeper into fuller sounds. That's just another way of saying, based on the way the human hearing systems works, you'll hear more of the spectral content with a full sound than you would hear with a thin sound. A full sound is not necessarily a loud sound. Tune the audio level just below your personal threshold level of loud, and remember that loudness threshold levels vary according to fundamental frequencies, spectral content, spectral component action, as well as your personal preferences at the moment. And those preferences are subject to any number of different variables—time of day, your age, your health, your state of mind, your experiences with sound and imagery, your hormone levels, etc. Of course those principles must be balanced with the psycho-physical need to avoid the discomfort of continuous full sounds; bear in mind that the duration of the sound is another variable that effects the tuning of the amplitude level.

Also, search for the sweet spot in the stereo audio field, a spot found near the apex of an equilateral triangle formed by you and the stereo speakers. When you find that sweet spot, slowly turn your head from side to side to make it easier to perceive the connections between phase changes in the audio and movement in the light forms. There's much to be learned here about the connections between psychoacoustics and psychooptics. Getting a sense of the common ground shared by hearing and seeing should be one of the benefits of working with these visual music studies.

Furthermore, remember that the material on Part Two: The DVDs is a media translation of the original mode of presentation. There are significant size and quality differences between the original projected laser light forms and the video light forms you'll be witnessing from the DVDs. Additionally, for the video, gamma adjustments to tone down the mid tones were made to compensate for lack of contrast that creeps into the image via the steps of the media translation process. The first step in that translation chain involves the original laser projections on a screen being picked up by an analog S-VHS video camera which is patched to an S-VHS analog video tape recorder for recording to analog videotape. The material on the analog videotape is then translated to digital videotape. The material on the digital videotape is then transferred to a computer. Finally the material is translated to MPEG, the DVD format for the storage of video. That final version of the material is a very long way from the original experience.

It's a high tech wonder that the material on these DVDs remains relatively intact. It's also a testament to just how forgiving our perceptual systems are. The downside for beginners is that your memory system can't help you fill in the perceptual gaps if you've never had similar experiences in the past; there's no filler data available in your memory to be brought into play. Thus, as you experience these DVDs without the benefit of memories of similar past experiences, you're truly on the edge of realtime as it cuts its way through the experience—throws some doubt on whether the first time is always the best.

FOUR

Pythagoras & Pellegrino In Petaluma

20
Pythagoras In Petaluma

Pythagoras of Samos, a mystical, mathematical, and acoustical philosopher, who along with his followers in the 6th century BC and beyond, set the stage for the development of psychophysics (the physics of the senses) in the present day. Why is Pythagoras in Petaluma over 2500 years after his lifetime? The answer to that question is that the spirit and the thought of Pythagoras are and have been for decades the driving forces for my work found on DVD volumes 3 and 4 of these studies. My studies of the work of Pythagoras began in an undergraduate philosophy class at Lawrence University in 1959 and continued in the mid 1960s in graduate philosophy and history of music theory classes at the University of Wisconsin—Madison.

Beginning in 1974 the work seen and heard on DVD volumes 3 and 4 was developed in my personal studios and various institutional studios I developed and directed over the years. Research grants from Oberlin College and the National Endowment for the Humanities were particularly helpful in the early stages of this work. Finally it was in my Petaluma studios in the 1980s and 1990s that this work was refined and recorded. The sounds and images emerged from principles laid out by Pythagoras and his school 2500 years ago.

The key principle in these particular visual music studies is that both the laser animations and music emerge from precisely the same stereo wavetrains—the sound and the light forms are radiations of one and the same flowing electrical energy. The stereo wavetrains are tuned on-the-fly and played in realtime according to Pythagorean principles. Those principles are fundamental to the poetics of dynamics, the art of articulating and moving through time by creating animated laser light forms, a form of visual music, and in these particular examples, the music of fundamentally integrated sound and light.

Pythagoras was the inspiration for a community of mathematical mystics who flourished in southern Italy during the fifth century B.C. He was a true peripatetic working several hundred years before Aristotle. Before he settled in southern Italy he traveled widely with his father in various cities of the Greek empire—in Egypt, in Syria, in Phoenicia, in Babylonia, and in India. During his travels, he studied with various influential philosophers and teachers including Thales and Anaximander. In his day, philosophy was the study of the science of mathematics, music, art, literature, astronomy, and cosmology, what in the early 21st century might be called a liberal arts education. So it should come as no surprise that the educational background of Pythagoras was well tuned for him to become a master integrator.

Pythagoras held that the dynamics of world structure depended upon the interaction of contraries, or pairs of opposites. In other words, he was referring to the generative principle of a difference in potential, the condition that creates the force that generates the electrical waveforms that give rise to the sound and light forms on these DVDs as well as to the life forms that might study these DVDs. He also held that all existing objects were fundamentally composed of form and relationships and not of material substance; it's worth noting, that's a modern lesson taught today by quantum physics.

Modern physics is about discovering and formulating the laws that govern transformations all along the continuum from the smallest to the largest physical structures. What fuels those transformations is the push/pull forces generated by differences in potential, forces such as energy, momentum, and electrical charge. One of the purposes of these visual music studies is to make those forces palpable in ways that contribute to a deeper understanding of how such transformations work across media and across our modes of perception.

The material on these volumes represents one demonstration after another of the Pythagorean principle that what gives form to the Unlimited is the Limit. The Unlimited here is represented by the infinite continuum of potential frequency ratios and the Limit is represented by whole number frequency ratios. And remember, harmony, according to most music theorists and psychophysicists, is based on whole number frequency ratios. On these volumes it's the whole number frequency ratios that provide the underlying structure for these visual music studies, just as they do for most music, past and present.

A notion to bear in mind is that every sound/light image, however fleeting, has numerical attributes that uniquely describes it, and that's true of all sound/light images on and off these volumes. At its most fundamental level the science of any field is based on numbers generated by an arbitrarily agreed upon metric system; that metric system is logical only after the fact. If something is too small to be measured, it's nothing, or maybe a figment of someone's imagination, a theory at best. A thing doesn't exist until someone invents a metric system sensitive enough to sense it and measure it, and then out of nothing it becomes something with a name and with a value. A good approach to the history of science is to track the history of inventions (such as metric systems) that have given us conceptual or physical tools that sharpen, deepen, and extend human sensory functions.

Personally I've found these sounds and images helpful in getting insight into the relationships of numbers and how nature generates forms from numbers. The forms in these studies are ephemeral in their natural state, but if they were created with different energy systems the forms would change into what we recognize as matter. What I found seductive from the beginning was how these sounds and images managed to both carry and evoke human feelings. And that made a very good fit with what I'd learned from years of studying Suzanne Langer's work, the essence of which I'd capsulize as the expressive power of the resonance that emerges between similar dynamical systems. In a nutshell, that's what people are referring to when they say that "the music moved them"—in other words, that the structure of the music's dynamical system was close enough in form to generate in them corresponding human feelings. The resonance is in their sensory system as well as their entire being.

Since my introduction to his work I felt an immediate kinship with Pythagoras; that happened when I first studied his thought as an undergraduate in a philosophy class at Lawrence University in 1959. That feeling only got stronger as I did graduate studies in philosophy, and then, for over three decades, continued my self-guided philosophical studies while at the same time found myself steeped in visual music research and composition. In fanciful moments I also sense a genetic connection, if not directly to Pythagoras then possibly to someone in his community. My mother and father were both born in southern Italy and their ancestors have deep roots in that region, so it's not that much of stretch for me to imagine my genetic line going back to the days when the Pythagoreans were flourishing in southern Italy.

The influence of Pythagorean thought extends through later Greek philosophers into modern science, an encompassing field based on the Pythagorean notion that all things are numbers. The Pythagoreans, in exploring the physics of vibrating strings, concluded that harmony was tied to the phenomenon of simple whole number frequency ratios. In these particular visual music studies whole number frequency ratios are easy to see and hear; they result in clearly defined, relatively static or very slow moving laser images and relatively uncomplicated sounds.

The music synthesizer generated stereo wavetrains that create the sounds and images start out on two separate paths. Along the way they are sometimes subjected to separate modulation signals, in effect, other wavetrains or cross currents that influence their natures. Farther down the path both original wavetrains may also be subjected to exactly the same modulation signal. Even farther down the path the wavetrains may be merged or mixed in varying degrees. Every step from beginning to end is micromanaged in protocompositional design and micro-tuned on-the-fly according to what's being seen and heard at the moment. It's worthwhile to note that small changes in wave train variables often lead to large consequences both in the sound and the light forms (a key principle of Chaos Theory).

These visual music studies are about integral connections, meaning both integers and integration. And that's exactly what concerned the Pythagoreans—the connections between integer ratios, that is, whole number ratios and harmony. From the simplest to the most complex architectures in most music, harmonious intervals are the basic building materials. That fact is as true today as it was 2500 years ago in the time of Pythagoras. The point of this area of my visual music research is that those same integral principles provide the integrative connections between dynamic imagery and sound, the laser light forms and the music.

For more information, see Chapter 21, titled Laser Animations and Pythagorean Thought.

21
Laser Animations
And Pythagorean Thought

My work with laser animations is rooted in Pythagorean thought. In terms of the theory I'm late on the scene; Pythagoras had the theory worked out thousands of years ago. However, what he did not have in his day were the electronic instruments we have today, in particular the oscilloscope and the laser animation system. By means of my oscillographic and laser animation work I've been searching for a common ground for the ear and the eye, for sound and sight.

What I discovered was that when tuned appropriately, a stereo wave train will produce harmonious sound and imagery that together provide insight into the natural order of things—in this case that frequency ratios composed of single digit whole numbers will produce sounds and images that are naturally harmonious. Ratios with smaller numerical values and involving multiples with smaller numerical values are the most harmonious. Dissonance gradually increases as the numerical values increase.

The smaller the numbers in the ratios, the greater the audio consonance, the simpler the image. 1:1 is a unison. 2:1 is an octave. 3:2 is a perfect fifth. 4:3 is a perfect fourth. 5:4 is a major third. 6:5 is a minor third. 7:6 is a minor third that seems a bit too small to the ear accustomed to equal temperament. 8:7 is a major second that seems a bit too large. 9:8 is a major second. When all these ratios are perfectly tuned, their corresponding images are perfectly stable. The images increase in complexity as the numbers in the ratios increase in value; the same is true for the sound. Using the preceding list of ratios, 1:1 produces the simplest (most consonant) sound and the simplest image and 9:8 produces the most complex (relatively dissonant) sound and the most complex image.

Deviations in tuning around those whole number ratios create movement in both the sound and the image. Human contrivance comes into play when I note and study the conditions for returning to my personal preferences and playing with whatever it takes to get from one ratio to another in an aesthetically effective way. Engaging in the process of noting, studying, and playing is what I'm referring to when I call these pieces Visual Music Meditations. From another perspective it would be just as accurate to refer to the pieces as studies. But I prefer calling them meditations because of the state of mind this work tends to cultivate.

Commonly when I do this sort of work I find myself in a state where the soul seems freed from the body, so that rational apprehension takes on the character of immediate perception, intuition in its most fundamental form. For me this process has served educational functions from the most elementary to the most elevated levels. To document my meditations I have to bootstrap myself to enter a disciplined, linear state of mind in order to write notes, make flowcharts, configure recording equipment—whatever it takes to set the stage for a return to the material sometime in the future. I view the necessity of documenting meditations as a form of harmonizing Pythagorean contraries—in this case, the rational and the intuitive.

The Pythagoreans considered numbers as being represented and incorporated in concrete physical forms including geometrical figures. What I create with my laser animations are not concrete physical forms; rather they're ephemeral forms that create the illusion of fluid physical forms often reminiscent of natural concrete physical forms. Technically the imagery belongs in the realm of Lissajous figures, the expression named after Jules A. Lissajous, a 19th century French physicist credited with the concept of creating curves in one plane traced by a point (the laser or the electron beam) moving under the influence of two separate harmonic motions (stereo wavetrains in my work). Lissajous invented a device that employed mirrors attached to tuning forks so aligned that light striking one mirror would also be reflected off the other mirror. If the vibrating forks were tuned to harmonic intervals (small number integer ratios) the light reflected by their mirrors onto a wall would have basic shapes similar to what my laser animation system produces.

Anyone who's taken a physics class has probably seen common examples of Lissajous figures generated by simple harmonic motions, perpendicular to each other, with a simple frequency ratio; you won't find those images in my work. My laser animation work tends toward the farther reaches of the Lissajous figure realm, and my emphasis is on musical movement and metaphorical forms rather than the measurement techniques used in the physics lab for sound and radio signals. All my imagery and sounds are created by continuous streams of numbers but my preferred approach to the process is to sense the streaming numbers rather than calculate them. Like most processes in the arts, the streams and relationships of numbers that create my laser animations could be calculated and analyzed after the fact. And, from time to time, when I'm in a linear mode, I'll stop to do some calculations and analysis. I'll do that mainly because it provides another perspective on the designs, an additional view that might lead to the discovery of one or more wrinkles for improving the design, or possibly lead off into unexplored territory.

There are sites on the internet that let you experiment with Lissajous figures to come up with a variety of images. They are both enjoyable and edifying as far as they go. They are particularly good for giving you an idea of how different frequency ratios generate different images. The downside to the sites I've visited is that they present theoretical concepts unaccompanied by compositional tools. In other words, what they are presenting is similar to a simple listing of the intervals two melody instruments might play in a duet; but what you don't get is the compositional or performance tools to create the process of getting from one interval to another over time. Critical musical variables such as rhythm and dynamics are not to be found. Amplitudes are geared to fit the images into a defined display area. The frequency ratios flip discretely from one set to another with no easing in nor out of ratios. In some cases you're allowed to adjust phase changes by incrementing or decrementing the frequency of one signal or another, but you can't play it musically the way you can with a music synthesizer driven deflection system.

Compared to what you're likely to find on the internet and see on your computer display, what makes a laser animation system, an electromechanical system, particularly valuable as a visual music instrument is that its mechanical characteristics make it more akin to traditional music instruments, instruments that carry an expressive history. Each unit of the laser animation system is composed of a mirror attached to the arm of a galvanometer. Each unit has frequency and amplitude limits as well as resonant frequencies, just like every acoustic instrument. As any instrumentalist would agree, learning to play within the limits of their instrument and pushing against those limits is a major part of learning to play the instrument; and the same is true of getting a sense of how to adjust to those areas where an instrument either over-responds or under-responds. Playing a laser deflection system requires the same sort of sensitivity to instrumental idiosyncrasies as playing an acoustic instrument.

In the final analysis, there's considerable value in exploring the internet sites that give you access to Lissajous figures because you'll come away with an experiential base for understanding the foundation for music driven laser animations. But bear in mind that the laser animation system is far more complex and sophisticated than any system you're likely to find online. Online you'll find a laboratory demonstration device whereas the laser animation system is a music instrument.

It's worth noting that although all my laser animations in performance mode result from frequency ratios, not all of them are accompanied by the sounds of those frequency ratios. Some laser animations do emerge directly from the music, whereas some are created as interpretations of the music, and still others are counterpoints to the music. As you might expect, DVD volumes 3 and 4, entitled Pythagoras & Pellegrino In Petaluma, include only pieces involving laser animations that have one-to-one correspondences with the sounds that accompany them. Laser animations serving as interpretations of, or counterpoints to the music can found on DVD volumes 1 and 2 in any of the pieces that include SR HP (from the Santa Rosa Hewlett-Packard session) in their titles.

22
The Laser Animation System

The visual images are produced by a specially designed electromechanical optical system for deflecting a laser beam—very lightweight mirrors superglued to small posts on galvanometers. Galvanometers are small motors that translate the electronic wavetrains of a synthesizer to mechanical vibrations that drive the small posts on the galvanometers. The vibrating mirrors on the posts are positioned to provide deflection of a laser beam along the x and y axes, and then to project the resulting image out onto a screen or any other reflective surface. My laser animation system is configured so each galvanometer has a different frequency range as well as different sets of resonant frequencies; such a configuration ensures that the system as a whole behaves much like a music instrument, in this case a visual music instrument.

This is a system I designed in 1974, first to augment and then finally to replace the instrument (the oscilloscope) I had been using since 1967 for my music synthesizer generated oscillographic images. From 1971 to 1973 the images from the oscillographic system were translated to a set of 16 mm films called the Lissajous Lives Film Series. The oscillographic films were used in a variety of ways—as dynamic graphic scores to be interpreted by performers on any combination of instruments and as set pieces with composed scores including both electronic and acoustic instruments. Many times during the 1970s and early 1980s, as part of my visiting artist engagements at universities and art museums, I used the oscillographic films as dynamic graphic scores to be interpreted in concert with local musicians. Friends in other music groups used my films in similar ways. The Blackearth Percussion Group toured Europe and the USA with one of those films. Phil Rehfeldt of Clarinet and Friend toured the USA a number of times with another one of those films built into a piece I composed for him called Phil's Float.

The physical limits of this particular laser animation system are defined by the frequency ranges of the galvanometers, the use of an off-the-shelf audio power amplifier to process the wavetrains that drive the galvanometers, and the nonlinearity of the galvanometers. The nonlinear response of the galvanometers results in a number of narrow bands of highly responsive resonant frequencies, as well as gradual drop-offs in response at the lower and upper ends of the frequency range. Within those physical limits full use is made, both individually and in combination, of the various electronic wave modulation types available on the Synthi AKS synthesizer, including amplitude, frequency, waveshape, and phase modulation.

As a visual music instrument the laser animation system has served a variety of presentation and performance functions—sometimes solo especially in the demonstration mode, sometimes in ensemble with other performance artists including musicians, dancers, and light artists, and sometimes being picked up by a video camera and routed to a computer for realtime processing and video projection.

To compose the pieces for the two DVDs called Pythagoras & Pellegrino In Petaluma (Volumes 3 and 4), I designed a configuration that ensured I would only be using animated laser imagery that worked within the limitations of the video medium. In a nutshell, I played my Synthi AKS to drive my laser animation system so that it's imagery was projected onto a screen. The imagery was picked off the screen by a video camera whose output was split out to a test video monitor and a video recorder which was also recording the synchronized sound from a split off the Synthi AKS.

What you see on the DVDs is a subset of what's possible with my laser animation system. One of the earliest lessons you learn as a composer is to understand the principles of idiomatic writing, to work with the strengths and within the limitations of an instrument or combination of instruments. The desire to record some of my animated laser imagery was enough of a spur to bring that old lesson back to the surface. It helped me overcome my customary urge to show my audience the farther reaches of the system, best seen in live performance. I spent so many years believing that it was not in my best interests to record my laser work that I had thoroughly programmed myself to avoid the rigors associated with actually doing the recording. Truth be told, the refining and recording process was considerably more enjoyable than I anticipated. I should have know better. Freedom can also be a spoiler.

For the material on these DVDs, the synthesizer generating the wavetrains is a Synthi AKS, an early 1970s hybrid synthesizer with analog wave functions and a digital keyboard. I'm working with patches or higher level circuit designs that I've been refining since the mid 1970s. The tuning of the synthesizer's individual wave functions is done by hand control via potentiometers addressing the various wave functions. The hand controls include highly sensitive five-turn potentiometers for fundamental frequencies and somewhat less sensitive one-turn potentiometers for controlling amplitude, waveshape, phase, low-pass filter cutoff frequency, and mixing. In addition, a scalable two-axis joystick can be patched to control any wave variable.

What makes the Synthi AKS especially good for playing the role of wave train generator is its use of a patch matrix rather than patch cords for internal communication and controls. All the inputs and outputs of every Synthi AKS function are made available by the the ingenious design of a centrally placed patch matrix that incorporates input and output busses along vertical and horizontal axes. All that's required is a patch pin to connect the output of one function to another function's input; that operation can happen very quickly. It's clean. It's fast. And once one is accustomed to viewing the matrix, it's easy to understand a design or a patch at a glance. Consequently, the Synthi AKS is a perfect instrument for playing a laser animation system. Nevertheless, any electronic system capable of generating precisely controllable stereo wavetrains in the audio range would be a good experimental candidate for driving a laser animation system.

23
The Laser Images

The laser images are drawn out over time by a deflected point of laser light following paths prescribed by the interaction of the stereo wavetrains driving the mirrors via their galvanometers. In perceptual terms, the physical creation of the forms is based on the persistence of vision, a psycho-optical phenomenon characteristic of the human visual system that results in sustaining an image for a short time after its cause is removed. When creating the images it's not much of a challenge for me to tune to the human visual system because I just rely on my own visual system, figuring that most interested parties, given even a short learning curve, will see much of what I see in the images, especially when I verbally guide their eyes in demonstrations.

However, the video visual system presents special problems because rather than taking the visual information in a continuous flow, it breaks it into 29.97 frames per second. Furthermore, each of those frames is made up of two fields which can be thought of as sub-frames that address alternately the odd and the even lines of the video screen, a process that's called interlacing. So, in recording to video, an initially unbroken laser flow becomes chopped by the video recording system into frames and fields, and that chopping presents two separate frequency obstacles (around 30 Hz, the frame rate, and 60 Hz, the field rate).

Those video obstacles or limitations must be factored into the design of acceptable, recordable laser images; that factoring process is best done by eye, by making the final decisions on whatever you're trying to capture by viewing the imagery on a video monitor while you're creating it. The point is that given all the restrictions of a video visual system—frames, fields, aspect ratio, screen size, all the variables connected with light generation which includes dot size, phosphors or liquid crystals, etc.—it's important to remember that the images that finally made their way to the DVDs in this project are a relatively small sample of what's possible with my laser animation system in a full size projection mode. A full size projection mode can fill any size screen, or reflect off multiple screens set at different angles and locations, or expand and stretch in ways that makes the imagery crawl along the walls or the ceiling. Despite the limitations of media translation there's still much to be learned about visual music from the contents of a DVD.

The laser images with clearest definition and greatest stability are the result of stereo wave train fundamentals with whole number ratios. In other words, for maximum definition and stability the ratio of the frequency of the wave train on the x-axis to the frequency of the wave train on the y-axis might be 3:2 or 4:3 or 7:1 or some other whole number ratio. The slightest deviations from whole number ratios create movement in the laser image. The smaller the deviation, the slower the movement. **Performance is a type of realtime composed walking tour through various states of dynamic equilibrium found around the intersections of fundamentals with whole number ratios.** Absolute equilibrium (perfect for cadences) is found at the intersections. The realtime compositional process can be thought of as a dance to, from, and around those intersections.

Numerous other design principles also come into play. For example, the more complex the ratios, the more complex the images. Likewise, the more complex the waveforms, the more complex the images. Often very small changes in wave variables result in very large changes in images especially at the intersections and as the fundamentals zero-in on, as well as pass through, the resonant frequencies of the galvanometers. The art of moving from one intersection to another and dancing around those intersections in terms of the fine tuning adjustments of frequency, amplitude, waveshape, and phase is what breathes life into the performance process. It is in this context that the meaning of dynamic equilibrium becomes clear. Perfect equilibrium all the time would be perfectly boring because there would be no movement, no life to the sound and light forms. Dynamic equilibrium is expressed as the nature of the movement to, from, and around the intersections of the whole number ratios.

For additional information see my second book, *The Electronic Arts of Sound and Light* (1983), which includes a chapter called Laser Light Forms. That chapter presents my thinking on the subject up to 1981. That book also includes a series of relatively high resolution photos of laser images in color. The sort of images seen there, because they include such fine detail, do not lend themselves to being captured by the comparatively lower resolution video systems; so the laser imagery seen on my DVDs is in a special class. In terms of performance, the classes are very similar; the differences are in the graphic details that are available to be captured by film and by video, the differences between higher resolution (film) and lower resolution (video).

24
Animated Laser Visual Music Meditations

In a related and abbreviated form this chapter appears on my website. It's included here because it covers details not found in other parts of this book.

The Root Idea:
- Playing with visual music/sonification, a focused multimedia approach based on natural and invented visual connections, reflections, translations, mappings, and embodiments of music
- Exploring dynamical wavetrains/data trains that work aesthetically for both the ear and the eye.
- Searching for a common ground for the ear and the eye.

The Context:
- I've been exploring the audiovisual, cross-modal electronic arts field since 1967 when (as part of a doctoral project at the University of Wisconsin) I hung an oscilloscope on the end of the wavetrains emerging from a Moog synthesizer to begin to understand the connections between the Moog's electronic transfer functions and what I was hearing from the speakers. My career in visualizing music had an unintentional beginning. Because there were no instructional materials available in 1967 for the Moog synthesizer, I was forced to learn the instrument by my own devices, which happened to include speakers for listening and an oscilloscope for looking. Instruments soon to follow were four-channel oscilloscopes, spectrum analyzers, film cameras, video cameras, audio and video synthesizers, laser animation systems, video and data projectors, special purpose computers, general purpose computers, and the complete range of audio recorders.
- My focus is ongoing research in the electronic arts of sound and light with applications in multimedia performance art, communications, and education.
- The process includes realtime performance-multimedia events based on my continuing experiments in the integration of the physics, psychophysics, and metaphysics of sound, light, form, and movement.

Applications:
- Public performance-multimedia events in universities, art museums, science museums, and cultural centers for the purpose of scattering idea seeds for visual music and sonification.
- Demonstrations and publications for professional groups.
- Expositions on my website.

One of the Systems for Realizing the Idea: The System for Animated Laser Visual Music Meditations:

1. Stereo wavetrains/data trains are generated by a hybrid stereo synthesizer capable of realtime control of frequency modulation, amplitude modulation, waveshape modulation, ring modulation, and phase modulation.

2. One branch of the stereo wavetrains/data trains:

    a) is routed through an affordable stereo amplifier that drives an xy laser deflection/projection system producing performable laser animations on a projection surface;

    b) and simultaneously a second branch is routed downline directly to an audio mixer;

    c) and simultaneously a third branch is routed to the Fairlight Voicetracker.

3. The laser animations are picked up by a S-VHS video camera that is connected to an Amiga computer which digitizes and processes the video for recording to a S-VHS video deck in synchrony with the audio manifestations of the same wavetrains/data trains that produce the laser animations.

4. One audio leg is routed to a Fairlight Voicetracker, a special purpose computer for analyzing and converting audio frequency, amplitude, waveshape, and duration to MIDI signals.

5. The MIDI signals control and conduct a networked orchestra of MIDI synthesizers programmed to respond to the MIDI signals that pass through adjustable response windows defined as upper and lower thresholds for frequency, amplitude, and duration.

6. The second stereo audio leg is routed to an audio mixer to be mixed with the outputs of the MIDI orchestra and then recorded to S-VHS tape in synchrony with the video of the laser animations.

The Systems Game:

If used alone, all instruments, including synthesizers (notwithstanding all that marketing hand-waving about infinite possibilities), impart their inherent sound and light signatures on any work created with them. The only way an electronic artist can create a truly unique voice with commercial or custom products is to combine instruments into one-of-a-kind performance/production systems. Such a performance/production system is, in fact, a higher level instrument much like the traditional orchestra can be considered an instrument. And just as the orchestra, such systems can be used for a variety of pieces with very different results. The system described above was recently used in a piece, **Air Time**, that featured four young girls playing on a trampoline that functioned as the animation and audio generators and triggers; the dynamics of their play figured into shaping the work rather than using electronic control systems (pots, switches, keyboards, etc.) customarily built into synthesizers. A project in process, Nonstop, uses the same system with the nonstop action of a kid's soccer match as the structural control input.

Since it takes years to build a subtle performance technique, I leverage that time investment by integrating older instruments with newer instruments in ever-changing systems configurations so as to create unique higher level systems for performance-multimedia. The instruments included in the system described above cover an acquisition period of over three decades; worth noting is that it makes good sense to keep and use the tools in which you've made a life investment (considerable time and probably significant cash). If you spend enough time with instruments, and that includes defining instruments as various combinations of hardware and software, they simultaneously influence your thinking and become extensions of it. For as long as you intend to be active in the electronic arts field it is not a good idea to abandon instruments. Why cut yourself off from resources in which you invested significant portions of your life? Instead figure out how to integrate the resources into your current thinking or hold them in reserve so they are available for use should the muse beckon. This argument holds that bringing as much as possible of your history to bear on the moment will only enrich and deepen your work, and that includes the history you have with various instruments.

FIVE

DVD Volume 1

DVD Volume 1
Set One:
1. Winter Reflections

Winter Reflections was composed during the last week of 1998 and the first of 1999 in the main MIDI studio of Electronic Arts Productions. Like many other people at that time of the year I tend toward a reflective mood, so I was in the midst of composing a video piece (Winter Reflections on the Sweetness of Youth) based on the joyful movement of children at play on a perfect summer day—dancing in circles, twirling in pairs, and running after each other up, down, and over a redwood deck. It was the sweetness and innocence of their play that inspired the music for this piece. Originally it was intended as a score for that video piece. But as so often happens with the work of composers who take a modular approach to their work, the music found a number of different dancing partners including this video work. The imagery you see on this video may seem a long way from the children at play, but that's not the case from my perspective, because I often view groups of playing children as more abstract sets driven by nature's dynamical systems algorithms.

The music of Winter Reflections could have been and could still be completely notated in the traditional way. However what I did instead was to work with a realtime compositional process that I've been developing since my early years in music. This time the process involved designing an orchestra that I could conduct and play in realtime. Concurrent with that particular instance of the design process, I was experimenting with melodic, harmonic, and rhythmic structures that could have been committed to a traditional compositional sketch pad, but what I did instead was to literally air the ideas, sculpt them in realtime, and record them for study and development.

Over an extended series of days I revisited the process until the piece assumed its natural shape. By natural shape I mean that the musical ideas would find their authentic shapes and relationships naturally if they were aired and considered often enough; the thinking is similar to what novelists mean when say that they let the characters in their work speak in their own voices rather than forcing them to speak in voices fabricated by the author—it's a matter of finding rather than forcing the voices. One of the benefits of the realtime compositional process is that it greatly reduces the division between creating and editing, often to the point where they are indistinguishable. Plus if you love being in the company of the actual sound of your work, this compositional process is a wonderful way to work. The sound leads the way if you have the ears to follow.

The imagery was composed with ArtMatic, software that gives the user access to dynamical system algorithms represented in the user interface as a set of selectable flowcharts composed of selectable mathematical functions. The software is beautifully designed to encourage the user to experiment with complex dynamical systems at multiple levels (structures, functions, and parameters) and gives one almost instant visual feedback on what happens when the algorithms are modified, the functions are rearranged, and/or parameters are fine-tuned. When I work with generative software (ArtMatic belongs to that class) I make a concerted effort to avoid the use of its identifying or signature features. Instead, whenever I work with any piece of hardware or software, generative or not, what I do is to seek out and explore its quirks, odd turns, cracks, anomalies, and other oddities, and then let those strange twists lead me to unanticipated suggestions for pieces. Then the process becomes a game of playing with the most seductive leaders, and finally settling with the most musically satisfying of the group.

DVD Volume 1
Set One:
2. The Unison

The Unison is from Visual Music Meditations, a set of video pieces with my music and music synthesizer generated laser animations that have their roots in my earliest explorations of music synthesizers dating back to 1967. From 1967-1975 I hung an oscilloscope on the ends of music synthesizer wavetrains as a vehicle for exploring the nature of the synthesizer and eventually, in 1971/72, for composing a series of five films called the Lissajous Lives Film Series. In effect, during those years I was seeing what I was hearing and hearing what I was seeing since both the imagery and the sound were derived from one and the same source, namely the electronically generated wavetrains. At that time the oscilloscope was one of my most important tools for music visualization. Since there was virtually no instructional material on music synthesizers when I started in 1967, the oscilloscope was my main teacher and continued in that role for 8 years. Eventually, in 1975, I built a portable laser animation/projection system to use in addition to the oscilloscope for my electro-acoustic research. Performing on that laser system gradually replaced the films of oscillographically generated imagery in my performances.

Both the music and the imagery in The Unison are generated by the same source—stereo wavetrains I massaged in realtime with my Synthi AKS, an analog music synthesizer beautifully suited to the task. The musical "interval" of a unison is created by a 1:1 frequency ratio. In The Unison one of the ones in the 1:1 ratio has a more complex waveform than the other one; it's composed of additional harmonically related frequencies (whole number multiples of the fundamental) that give rise to the curls and loops in the imagery and the richness in the sound. The original form of the imagery was projected laser light animations captured by a video camera and recorded to videotape along with the audio signals generated by the music synthesizer. To achieve that end, the stereo output of the music synthesizer was split such that one stereo leg set was fed to the audio inputs of the video recorder while the other stereo set was simultaneously used to drive the laser animation projection system to produce imagery that was captured to videotape in synchrony with the audio leg.

The audio in The Unison was processed and polished in MetaSynth (a software synthesizer) so the piece would be more accessible beyond the inner circle of Pythagorean enthusiasts. The imagery was treated similarly in Premiere (video processing and editing software) so its appeal might also go a bit beyond the sphere of the purists. One of the purposes for composing The Unison was to put an excerpt of it on my website to give internet visitors a sense of what I meant when I wrote about the process for creating synthesizer-driven laser animations.

I did what I could to make the piece accessible on multiple levels and making the surface of the piece easy to take in is part of that plan. The fact is that I love the raw tapes as I love raw unprocessed food for its purity, but there's also as much to be said for the art of cooking electronic sound and light as there is for art of cooking food—cooked food carries the spirit of the cook blended with the spirit of the food, and so does cooked art, especially when it's cooked by the originator. But my raw food preference prevailed as evidenced by the inclusion in these Visual Music Studies of the two DVDs called Pythagoras & Pellegrino In Petaluma—those pieces involve no cooking.

In contrast to the electromagnetic purity of the oscilloscope, what I've always especially liked about the laser animation/projection system is that it behaves very much like an acoustic music instrument. Its personality is defined by very serious idiosyncratic nonlinearity, limits to its frequency range, predictable resonant frequency bands, and limits on how much driving force it can survive. In other words, it has its own particular visual voice just as every music instrument has its own particular sonic voice.

Beginning in 1975 I spent countless hours designing laser animation performance systems that I thought of as ragas and talas—collections of visual melodies, scales, tunings, and rhythms to be used in a realtime compositional mode. Which designs I used and how I used them were determined by the particular performance requirements of the engagement or session. Well into the late 1990s I was still fine-tuning and extending older designs and creating new ones.

Performance technique for creating laser animations requires a very light touch to the point of conceptually leaning on a control, such as a potentiometer, with my mind so as to make extremely small changes in phase, frequency, amplitude, and waveshape. In the first decade of my life as a music composer I studied all the acoustic instruments from the four principal orchestral families, often taking private instruction for years at a time to discover the idiosyncratic nature of every one of those acoustic instruments. In all those years I never encountered an instrument that requires a touch as subtle as an analog music synthesizer being used to create visual music. By far my favorite visual music synthesizer remains an analog instrument that arrived on the scene in the early 1970s, an instrument called the Synthi AKS. Its five-turn potentiometers for frequency control are as sweet as pots get—for the most delicate tuning adjustments you just touch the pot with your fingertips, think its rotational direction, and it moves every so slightly in response to your thought—I'm not exaggerating.

Numerous problems arise in the attempt to capture laser animations with a video camera, so despite the urgings over the years of some of my close colleagues, I resisted the idea of committing the animations to video. Nevertheless, late in the 1990s I decided to set apart a week to record to videotape the laser animations that would best fit the serious limitations of the video monitor—fixed aspect ratio, low resolution, miniscule window, among others. Much of what I've done since 1975 in the realm of laser animations is impossible to capture on videotape, so that material remains in the sphere of my live performances, what I do as part of my residency engagements. However, I was somewhat surprised by how many designs I could adapt to work reasonably well on video and many of those finds are included in DVD Volumes 3 and 4. My working title for that original set of video recordings was Visual Music Meditations; it was chosen because the required creative process is one of my doors to the meditative state.

Like so much of what I've done in the past, that set of video recordings took its place on a storage shelf waiting for the right time to be incorporated into a larger project. All the pieces in Pythagoras & Pellegrino In Petaluma, DVD Volumes 3 and 4 of *Emergent Music and Visual Music: Inside Studies*, are taken from the Visual Music Meditations set.

Eight hours after I posted an announcement, on a list devoted to the electronic arts, of the availability of an excerpt of The Unison I received the following email message from one of the artists ; she quickly managed to dial up the resonant frequency for this work:

To: uisoftware@topica.com
From: Diana Slattery <slattd@rpi.edu>
Subject: Re: UILIST: MS: The Unison
Date: Mon, 26 Mar 2001 04:23:51 -0800

Ron,

Strange thing to be doing at 7 in the morning, but what a treat. Saw an essay in generation of dimensionality. The one becoming the two; the two becoming three, and the three, moving to knot itself (illusionary) in four dimensional or higher space. Generation from primal tones. And the generation being fluid, not of discrete number-states, continuous.

If this can transmit the state of mind through the multiple mediations of computer, screen, small size--relative to the immersion of live performance, etc. -- the essential message penetrating layer upon layer of potential noise and translation, well--that's something else. Indeed.

The universe as a vast signaling system, built up from simple elements, which can always be recaptured, always underlie the greatest complexity of crisscrossing waves within waves.

Many thanks.

Diana Slattery

____ Original Message____

From: "Ron Pellegrino" <ronpell@microweb.com>
To: <uisoftware@topica.com>
Sent: Monday, March 26, 2001 3:18 AM
Subject: UILIST: MS: The Unison

>Fans of Pythagoras, that mystical, mathematical, and philosophical
>seminator from the 6th century BC, and those on the list who enjoy
>checking out music visualizations might find the latest post to my
>site of interest. I just posted The Unison, a video excerpt from a
>project of mine called Visual Music Meditations. Both the imagery

>and sound are derived from the same stereo wave train which in this
>excerpt is a unison finely tuned to create small but intimately
>coordinated sonically and visually significant changes in frequency,
>phase, amplitude, and waveshape. I used MetaSynth to polish and
>flesh out the audio leg of the wavetrains...

>Ron Pellegrino

Nine days after the posting of The Unison I received another response that I found, for different reasons, just as satisfying as the first one:

To: uisoftware@topica.com
From: Bob Seiple <seiple@gva.net>
Subject: Re: UILIST: MS: The Unison
Date:Wed, 4 April 2001 04:23:51 -0800

Ron,

I experienced Unison several times last night. I tried to enter into it, because I felt it would help me better know, if I could be a part of its unfolding. There was something large within its subtle changes which invited me to meet it. The next morning, I had a series of dreams, lucid dreams--probably at the edge of alpha. These dreams were successive small shifts-- approximations about a basic theme: there was a charcoal colored fish or lip shaped object, disc-like and containing hints of colors within its charcoal--a dull sheen of little rainbows. Actions or frequencies were streaming into this disc and different frequencies or harmonics were emanating out. I was "told" to come to know the process. It felt more than just a diminution of amplitude or change in frequencies. Something more dynamic and very sublime and perhaps magical was happening within this slender orb or Kleinfish. I felt that I was treated to experiencing some kind of learning to learn to learn to learn.

Thanks, Your Fellow In Alchemy, Squidpop

DVD Volume 1
Set One:
3. Cynthia's Dream

The title, Cynthia's Dream (1988), comes from the music, a set of three variations based completely on composer/performer Cynthia Fanning's voice recorded in the Texas Tech University's electronic music studio in 1980. At the time Cynthia was one of a group of outstanding musicians in my music composition class at Texas Tech (I taught electronic music, realtime composition, and founded and directed the Leading Edge Music Series at TTU from 1978-81). As a special project to be programmed on an annual contemporary music festival, she and I were collaborating on a performance piece based on the idea of musically inflecting and dramatizing the slightly varied meanings of the group of words listed under "unconformity" in *Roget's Thesaurus of Words and Phrases*. The recording was made as one of a set of loosening up exercises or studies for the purpose of discovering tools for her role in our performance piece. The recitation of her dream just emerged during the exploratory process; it wasn't scripted, it wasn't planned, and it wasn't anticipated. For years, because of the musical quality of Cynthia's delivery, I used the original unprocessed recording in my public presentations as an illustration of one of the flavors of visual music. Audiences loved it and I never tired of it. Just about everything Cynthia did was rich with musical flavors and the recitation of her dream is a perfect example.

Seven years later, in 1987, I began exploring the Fairlight Voicetracker, a special purpose computer that converts acoustic information (sound) into MIDI (music synthesizer digital control information). One of the areas I explored focused on examining the inherently musical nature of the human voice. What I discovered was that individuals have their own particular tonal centers, strong tendencies toward particular scale formations (seldom traditional scales), definite tempo and rhythmic predilections, characteristic melodic structures and ornaments, implied harmonic progressions (via arpeggiation), and spectral weightings. Moreover that whole list of musical variables is subject to change according to the time of the day, their moods, their health, their environment, the context, and other variables. Such findings didn't really come as a surprise because many musicians know those facts intuitively, but the Fairlight Voicetracker is a great tool for musically clarifying and illustrating those issues for anyone with ears to hear.

Every single note you hear in the music of Cynthia's Dream emerges in one way or another from Cynthia's voice on the recording. I transferred her voice to one track of a multitrack tape recorder. From there her recorded voice is connected to the Fairlight Voicetracker which, according to pitch, loudness, and tone color, converts the vocal sound into MIDI signals that are recorded by a computer software program called a sequencer. The computer software is used to process the MIDI signals in numerous ways—octave displacement, time displacement, and filtering by duration, intensity, and frequency level.

Running along with Cynthia's voice on the tape recorder was a synchronization track (SMPTE code) that was used to keep the computer and Cynthia's recorded voice moving along lock step. The MIDI signals coming out of the computer (synchronized to Cynthia's voice by the SMPTE track) were used to control and conduct an orchestra of music synthesizers specially programmed to work with Cynthia's voice. When the output of the synthesizer orchestra meshed with my emerging aesthetic criteria, it was committed to several of the tracks of the tape recorder. The final piece is a changing heterophonic mix of Cynthia's voice and the synthesizer orchestra it's conducting. If you listen closely you'll hear that, although some sounds might hit slightly before or slightly after Cynthia's words and be slightly higher or slightly lower in pitch than Cynthia, every single tone comes from her voice in heterophonic pulses, streams, and clouds.

The video is a live recording of one stream of what people witnessed of Cynthia's Dream during a live performance-multimedia event I produced at Illinois Wesleyan University in the early 1990s. Professor Jean Kerr is the dancer/choreographer on this video. From a set of my pieces I sent to her before my residency began, she chose to work with the music of Cynthia's Dream and experimented with it for weeks before I arrived on campus.

When I work with dancers I rarely impinge on their freedom to do as they like, so what you see her doing is all to her credit. My instructions to dancers are very basic—dance where I and the camera can see you, wear a light-reflective costume, and play in the light pools. To my eyes dancers are accomplished visual music instruments and when I play with them, it's as if we are in a music duet.

What you see in the video is the stream of the final video mix, just as it emerged from the performance-videography system that I was playing in realtime. What the audience was seeing in that performance was exactly that same stream on a video projector as well as multiple monitors distributed around the stage. Plus, of course, the audience saw the dancer working live. They also saw me playing the video camera on my shoulder with my right hand and the computer video digitizing and processing gear with my left hand. They could also see the three video monitors I was using in the pit for visual feedback on the various phases of the performance—one monitor for the output of the computer, another for the source video, and another for the final mix of the computer output and the source video.

There is no studio editing involved in this piece; it's all done in realtime. Performance-videography involves realtime video capturing, digitizing, and processing of musicians, dancers or other performance artists and then mixing those video streams on-the-fly with my pre-composed video animations, what I call source tapes. The source tapes are selected from an extensive collection with a broad expressive range; they are created and collected over the years with the intention that, whenever appropriate, a video will be selected to function as a source tape to be mixed with a live processed video stream in a performance mode.

DVD Volume 1
Set One:
4. Soft Candy

Soft Candy is a form of easy to take sweetness. On one level the piece is a bagatelle that I recorded as a reminder of the many hours of pleasurable play in my main Kelly Lane studio in Petaluma. That was my first dream studio. It was realized after over a decade of working in the dreary environments of institutional facilities often located in basements or interior spaces without fresh air or natural light. That particular dream studio had cathedral ceilings, skylights, openable windows on every wall for cross ventilation, a south side with large antique french windows looking out on a deck and a year-round garden, a projection room and, on the far wall, a huge projection surface for films and laser animations, plus plenty of room for multiple work spaces including an integrated analog/digital synthesizer setup and a library where I put the finishing touches on my second book *The Electronic Arts of Sound and Light*—nothing but fond memories of that space.

When I realized during the late 1980s that it was getting close to the time to leave the Kelly Lane studios and to make a move to the countryside, I decided to record some pieces that would function as mnemonics of that dream studio. Those pieces came quickly and easily and Soft Candy was one of them. For a few years before I recorded this piece I explored playing with, over, and against various metric grounds or environments that challenged the natural metric fallbacks of multiples of two and three. Soft Candy uses a meter of 13 which of course allows for a plethora of subdivisions—7 and 6, 8 and 5, 9 and 4, 5 and 5 and 3, and a host of their subdivisions such as 3 and 4 and 2 and 2 and 2, or 4 and 3 and 3 and 3, and so on. If you like to count, when you listen to this piece you'll hear the phrases emphasizing the 13 while flying freely and changing the subdivisions on-the-fly.

As any musician knows, practice makes perfect and, as I've told many parents, if your child doesn't love to practice, they don't have much of a future in music. The key to establishing a lifetime of effective practice is to figure out how to make it musically satisfying as well as challenging; one solution to that problem is to invent your own routines, etudes, or studies. Short of that approach you can always seek out what someone else has designed along those lines. As one of many such studies, Soft Candy made for sweet practicing.

Soft Candy was composed in 1988 with a system configured to behave like an orchestra or a media band. Since the late 1960s, one of my MOs as a composer/performer has been to collect electronic instruments born of different persuasions (west coast, east coast, keyboard controlled, wind driven, etc.) and to configure them into harmonious systems that make good learning and playing fields. As a composer, rather than forcing musical issues, I normally begin the compositional process experimentally searching for voices by coaxing my instruments to speak for themselves and to suggest musical paths for exploration and study.

Combining the voices of different instruments requires a sensitivity to the whole that results in nuanced adjustments to the individual voices to promote harmony within the collection in terms of spectral and time shapes as well as their functional roles in the overall scheme (lead, background, middle ground, etc.). Given sufficient time and consideration, the process of combining individual voices results in the emergence of a macro-voice, the voice of the orchestra. Numerous recorded test runs are an integral part of the process. The pick of the litter becomes the piece—always an intuitive call.

The imagery was performed in realtime to the music just as a dancer would move to the music. It was created on an Amiga 1000 using a mix of dynamic material from the Hewlett-Packard recording session, digitized photographic stills of cymatic processes, and a hand-painted sun symbol on a tile acquired while on a trip to southern Italy. The material from the Hewlett-Packard session is a duet of laser animation and video synthesis. The cymatic stills are treated to color cycling on the Amiga as is the Italian hand-painted sun.

DVD Volume 1
Set One:
5. Liquid Light

The music for Liquid Light is exactly the same music used for Soft Candy.

The title, Liquid Light, describes how it feels, literally by hand, to sculpt video light forms in visual music counterpoint to sonic music. The first section is created by entering into the light path between the camera and the video monitor with a small handheld magnifying glass and using it to play the video light stream in counterpoint to the music by virtually drawing the light out of the screen as if it were a viscous liquid. The last section illustrates how the video light in this feedback system responds to the human hand also as if the light were viscous liquid.

All the light manipulation is done by my left hand while my right hand is playing a video camera balanced on my right shoulder. The camera technique is one I've been exploring since the late 1980s when I added realtime videography to my performance-multimedia shows. In actual performances my left hand is just as likely to be manipulating a computer keyboard, a mouse, or switches and sliders of various pieces of video and audio gear while my right hand plays the video camera.

I was introduced to video feedback late in 1971 when I visited the National Center for Experiments in Television (NCET) at KQED in San Francisco in preparation for a research stint there funded in part through the generosity of faculty research support from Oberlin College. The artists at the NCET (and, I later discovered, other places) referred to feedback as a video whore—video feedback was technically easy to do so anyone could do it, thus the artistic value of anything done with it was greatly diminished in the opinion of insiders. I've never accepted that notion because the logic is flawed. Anyone can bang around on a piano but that doesn't devalue good piano performance. The same logic holds true for video feedback. Furthermore, especially in the early days, I often sensed the implicit desire of artists working with emerging technology to keep the circle of users as small as possible—the more exclusive the access to the technology, the more valuable the output of that technology, so their thinking goes. Flawed thinking again. A far more productive attitude is to make emerging technology affordable so more people can access it thereby enriching the field by adding their experiences and perspectives to the evolutionary mix. The upshot is not to let anyone discourage you from exploring video feedback systems or any other accessible instrument. The returns are manifold for the explorers.

The simplest video feedback system is a video monitor (A) and a video camera (B) cabled back to the video monitor (A). The monitor (A) generates light energy (photons) that are picked up the camera (B) then returned by cable to the monitor (A) to create a recurring loop (A to B to A to B to A etc.) of electronically generated light (emitted from the monitor) and electronically represented light (transduced by the camera into electronic signals).

The basic material (photons) of the loop is created by an electron gun, at the back of the video monitor, shooting an interlaced stream of electrons onto a phosphor coated glass surface (the screen of the video monitor). When struck by the electrons the excited phosphors emit photons (light particles/energy) that are picked up by the electric camera and routed back to the electron gun to perpetuate the loop.

Fluid dynamic light images are created via the video feedback process. In the simplest video feedback system the dynamic forms of the images are subject to combinations of fixed and continuously variable settings of the controls on the camera (focus, zoom, targeting, sensitivity, tilt, pan, etc.) and the monitor (brightness, sharpness, contrast, color settings, etc.) plus the distance between the monitor screen and the camera. More complex systems can be designed by adding physical objects and/or optics between the camera and the screen, as well as introducing electronic objects—circuits or algorithmic processes (computer hardware and software))—between the camera output and electron gun input—the monitor. The greater the number of objects added to the system, the greater the number of dynamic image possibilities.

In video feedback performance, light images are sculpted by playing sets of system variables, usually within well defined ranges previously determined by experimentation and aesthetic judgments. In effect, the sets become variations of a visual music instrument—virtual modules for creating visual music. And just like building skill on a traditional music instrument, intelligent practice on those virtual modules points in the direction of perfection, a notion best viewed as a cloud of possibilities from which one selects whatever is appropriate for the moment.

My personal inclination is to search for the "voice" of the system—what seems expressively natural for it. That search is an intuitive process of playing, tuning, and winnowing until the system gels in ways that generates desirable outputs. The emergence of such desirable outputs is the signal that the system is achieving a level of coherence that makes it performable (a very personal judgment and a skill that improves with time, thought, and practice).

There's a conversational quality about the process of video feedback that gives it added value for performance artists—especially in the early experimental stages when you're cultivating familiarity with the personalities of the instruments. Like music, the imagery spins out in time. Like music, its morphological context is determined by its recent history and probable future—what preceded it and what may possibly follow it. Contributors to the conversation are the video monitor, the video camera, the performer, any physical or electronic objects included in the system, and the psychological context (public performance, company of friends and family, solo exploration, etc.). The performer leads the conversation, but the other contributors (the gear) definitely have their own inclinations, in effect, their own minds. To make the creative process work, the performer must respect those minds and tune to the combination of their idiosyncrasies.

Since I added video to my visual music research in 1972, my video feedback systems have been used for compositional tuning exercises, for pure exploratory pleasure, and for demonstrations of how a fundamental life principle (feedback) can be a vehicle for performance art. They've also been integrated into my performance-multimedia systems.

Moreover, the feedback process is a karmic lesson demonstrating that where you've been and what you've done strongly influence where you're going and what you're going to do when you get there. In other words, the feedback process ephemerally embodies a memory integrated with its evolving form that strongly influences how that form will continue to evolve. To play the leading edge of that evolving form, you need to be conscious of what you've done to get there and of what the possibilities are beyond the edge of what you're doing—it's a tuning exercise in integrating past, present, and future.

There's a wonderful book, *THE LIVING ENERGY UNIVERSE*, that's packed from beginning to end with very convincing arguments for viewing the principle of feedback as the glue of life operating on all levels from the microcosm to the macrocosm—from quanta to farthest reaches of the universe. If you've managed to get to this point in this description, chances are very good that you'd find this book to be inspiring and enlightening.

DVD Volume 1
Set Two:
6. Windswept

The music for Windswept is an example of what I consider an orchestral environment. During the late 80s/early 90s I focused my audio work on orchestral designs based on multiple MIDI synthesizers configured and programmed to respond to various acoustic sound variables such as specific levels of frequency, amplitude, duration, and spectral content. MIDI recording and processing software were used on a Macintosh computer in such a way that windows with variable dimensions were employed to route and distribute control information to a collection of synthesizers functioning as the orchestra. So each synthesizer is an orchestral instrument in the same sense as the instruments in a traditional orchestra. That approach was a natural extension of the instrument design work I did in configuring the modules of analog synthesizers such as the large studio Moog and Buchla synthesizers that were my mainstays in the late 1960s and early 1970s.

The conductor in this case is a Casio Digital Horn with MIDI, the DH-100. My brief experiences with other wind controllers during the 1980s were never very satisfying so I temporarily put the wind controller idea aside. When Casio gave up on its Digital Horn and dumped them on the market for $50, I jumped at the opportunity to add their toy to my MIDI collection. It was in keeping with my signature lesson on the wisdom of working with affordable emerging technology in the arts; the DH-100 is an inexpensive instrument with great potential for any musician who has invested considerable time in developing a technique on any of the woodwind instruments. The DH-100 has the size and look of a soprano saxophone and its fingering patterns are close to it as well. Unlike an acoustic woodwind instrument, there is no vibrating reed; but it has a mouthpiece that reads your breath pressure, which is why it's called a wind controller and why the piece is called Windswept. I chose to explore the DH-100 as a master controller because for a long time I had been looking for a musically satisfying way to integrate my 19 years of serious clarinet study with my work in the electronic arts. With it I finally found a wind controller that worked so well that I was ecstatic for weeks on end.

Rather than notating the music in the traditional way I used the computer to record my DH-100 playing as realtime compositional sketches and to notate (record) all the musical variables as MIDI data—data that I could, after the realtime fact, study via the computer monitor. Of course a traditional score could have been printed out from that MIDI data but that would have been an unnecessary step since I did not intend for anyone else to perform this work. Instead my compositional efforts were directed toward experimenting with the fine tuning of variable windows (response ranges defined by MIDI parameters). I also experimented with the distribution of that control data out to a collection of synthesizers with particular voices that I tweaked to be responsive to it. The combination of that collection of synthesizers and their voices is the orchestra that is conducted by my playing of the DH-100.

Believe me, playing this game was a special thrill for someone who struggled for 19 years in the attempt to master what was possible with the sound world of a clarinet. Compared to the clarinet, playing the DH-100 greatly expands and enhances what's possible to do with your breath, your tongue, and your fingers. The music you hear on Windswept is the result of my playing in realtime. For example, I did not use any computer techniques to speed up data; what you hear is my actual tonguing speed which happens to be far faster than I could possibly play a keyboard controller. In fact, that tonguing speed may be just beyond the capabilities of a keyboard controller; that statement is based on the considerable experience I have with one of the best keyboards, a Roland A-80. My first clarinet teacher was a trumpeter (Pete Nicolai from Kenosha, Wisconsin) who was convinced it was a good idea for clarinetists to know how to double and triple tongue; most clarinetists in those days hadn't the faintest and even fewer do today.

Beyond the speed issue there's a matter of musical expression which is intimately connected with nuance, details so fine that they are virtually impossible to analyze logically. Such nuances are subliminal; they are what separates performance art from science based on measurement. That's not to say that it's absolutely impossible to measure every variable in a musical expression with the finest gradations currently possible, but rather, that the highest level of musical expression is different from performance to performance as well as from musician to musician; those subtle differences defy measurement. The analysis would be so complex that it would be aesthetically meaningless

What defines the performances of musicians is the indefinable—the particular subtleties and nuances that carry the human feelings generated and evoked by a particular performance by a particular musician. The main problem with machines, including computers and synthesizers, is to convince them to follow your dancing lead and to avoid allowing them to control your every move. Let's face the truth, we spend most of our time living in a world dictated by machines. But there are still those among us (I am one) who believe that the proper place of a machine in our lives is to extend our senses and to give us capabilities that we couldn't have without them, and that's how I make my way back to my use of the DH-100 as the conductor of the orchestra for this piece.

I've never been inclined toward motor music, mindless looping, or minimalist temple tapping/la-di-daing. Rather I tend toward music that's conversational in nature, music with phrasing that's shaped by the human breath so as to more naturally influence resonances in the audience. A wind controller makes that sort of musical shaping a breeze. Everything I have ever done musically is based on placing a high value on finding or creating shapes that are either sculpted by the breath or feel as though they are. So discovering an electronic tool that encouraged natural breath shapes was a special gift.

For humans there is built-in expressive power from any utterance that relates closely to the living voice, whether it be speaking, singing, shouting, screaming, and all the other sonic constructions the human voice is capable of generating. Wind instruments could just as easily be considered breath instruments, because without breath there would be no medium to carry the vibrations of lips, reeds, or edges of metal or wood. In terms of expressivity in music, there is an idiomatic problem with mechanical or electronic systems not influenced by the breath, because it is in their nature to have a continuous, unbroken source of pressure, whether it be air or its analog, electronic flow. Wind controllers such as the DH-100 present a solution to that problem; circular breathing aside, breaths are natural punctuation marks and natural energy envelopes. Plus, every one of us intuitively understands the biological significance of inhalation and exhalation, and, for the most part, are unconsciously moved by it.

At the heart of the process for creating the visuals for Windswept was an Amiga 1000, an inexpensive desktop computer that emerged in the mid 1980s and set the stage for the desktop multimedia revolution. Apple eventually picked up on the ideas Amiga introduced and developed, and somewhat later the PC world also jumped on the bandwagon. But the truth is that the Amiga was so far ahead of its time that it developed enough traction with multimedia artists that it was used well into the 1990s; and even in 2008 I still consider it a powerful visual music instrument in its own right, especially if you want to incorporate a retro look in your video mix.

Conceptually it allows for the integration of all the necessary ingredients for live videographic performance. Specifically it includes an input slot for a video digitizer that will convert the analog output of an analog video camera (the only affordable type available in the late 80s) to a digital signal; it also includes an input slot for a genlock such as the Super Gen that serves multiple video functions in realtime. Those functions include mixing in a variety of ways the live video camera feed processed by the Amiga with another video source. That video source could be a videotape of specially prepared material (a source tape), the output of another video camera, or the output of a video mixer processing multiple video sources.

The Amiga 1000 came to me as part of a compensation package for providing consultation services to a small startup company in the San Francisco North Bay called Euphonics International. This happened at the very beginning of the period when the entire North Bay, but especially the Petaluma Valley, was developing into a high tech area eventually known as Telecommunications Valley. All the big players were locating there, Hewlett-Packard built a second huge North Bay campus there, and many HP engineers, who for one reason or another left the HP fold, created startups along with many entrepreneurs new to the area. All that heady activity extended out to the apple orchards of Sebastopol, which is located midway between the North Bay and the Pacific Ocean, and that's where Euphonics was located, surrounded by Gravenstein apple orchards. For Euphonics the downside of all that sweetness, plus an income stream from products sold to Fairlight and Korg, was an exceedingly leisurely production schedule, which in the tech industry means the window of opportunity for sales will probably close before or very shortly after the product born of leisure is ready for market. And that's exactly what happened to the package we created, which meant we saw minimal cash returns.

Nevertheless, I certainly enjoyed the brainstorming sessions and the opportunity to work with a unique visual music instrument as it gradually assumed a workable shape. My job was to provide alpha-testing, to provide macrostructural and user interface guidance, and to write the first version of the instruction manual. This project involved a combination of software and hardware package, originally called Light Fantastic and eventually called Lightworks, that was being designed to facilitate live multimedia performance for public events such as rock concerts and other performance-multimedia events.

Over the years I've had numerous consulting gigs with companies like Buchla Associates, Texas Instruments, alphaSyntauri Corporation, and others. The job with Euphonics was by far the most interesting because it involved a small group, including a traditional painter and two software/hardware engineers, searching for ways to apply their tech talents and experience to the electronic arts of sound and light. What more could a I ask? A decent cash return on my time investment would have been welcomed. The project had been slogging around for a while before they contracted my services and, though the pace accelerated after I signed on, living the good life in California for the engineers seemed to undermine a business sense of urgency.

So one faces reality and plays the hand that's dealt. The cards that time included an unanticipated degree of difficulty in that the engineers were steeped in PC and mainframe thinking. Their idea of a user interface was a script—written commands to control every step of the way in a linear, logical fashion; clearly they had no experience in performance-multimedia where the moment is defined by art and not logic. In the performance arts logic has a strong position in preparation, but not in the actual performance where intuition reigns supreme.

One of my suggestions to them was to include the capability of using items from a set of stock functions to describe higher level operations (presets) and assign those presets to computer keys and/or specific MIDI data triggers. Once that design path is taken the range of possibilities expands very quickly because presets can be divided into subsets which can be combined to create new presets and the game goes on and on. Unfortunately we did not explore that path.

Nevertheless, the upside for me was that alpha-testing this project provided a rare testing ground for one type of integrative performance-multimedia, an art game I had already been playing for decades with whatever affordable technology I could find. Adapting to whatever the system was capable of doing was the standard operating procedure I used from the beginning of my art and technology explorations, so working with that package was no stretch at all. The composition of Windswept emerged, in combination with an accelerated Macintosh Plus, from the latter stages of the system we were developing. The Mac, via a recorded MIDI stream, actually conducted the Amiga running our experimental system. Like so many of my other compositions it was a test piece, a study, that had multiple performance functions. It gave the Euphonics group an idea of the state of the project at the time it was composed, and for years I used it in numerous concerts and lecture/demos while on tour.

After the Hewlett-Packard session, Windswept is the second earliest piece on this DVD set and it looks it—low resolution, color cycling, limited color range, etc. Windswept was actually completed in 1989. My earliest use of homegrown microcomputer graphics goes back to 1983, long before I started working with the Amiga. I used an Apple IIe for performance-videographics many times in public shows just to give people an idea of what was possible with microcomputers at that time and what was soon to come. The IIe uses an NTSC (standard video) output for its monitor so, of course, it will drive video monitors and video projectors. It's true that the Apple IIe's resolution was limited and so was the color range, but it was first on the affordable video scene and it was a fun box to boot. You can view imagery from a Paul Gleaves customized Apple IIe on all the pieces on DVD volumes 1 and 2 that begin with "SR HP" (Santa Rosa Hewlett-Packard campus).

DVD Volume 1
Set Two:
7. SR HP Flight 4

This excerpt was used many times over the years in my public lecture-demonstrations. It's a piece that came together early in the HP recording session and it has a quality that simply shoots me back to that time and place. The musicians were playing electric guitars and MIDI synthesizers in the earliest stages of the development of MIDI. Of special note is that, based on the sounds they made during this flight, the musicians were clearly familiar and comfortable with the historical roots of electronic music.

For more detailed information see Chapter 18, The Hewlett-Packard Session.

DVD Volume 1
Set Two:
8. Nina's Song

Debby Penberthy, at the time (1999) a graduate student at the University of Wisconsin—Madison, is the vocalist and music composer. Mary Darcy, an undergraduate, is the dancer. I did the performance-videography; for a detailed description of performance-videography see the last two paragraphs of the notes on Cynthia's Dream. The performance was included on one of the public events I produced there as part of a week-long residency in 1999.

This is a recording of a live performance with nobody at the recording controls. One leg of the combined audio/video—also distributed to multiple video monitors, a projector, and speakers—was patched into a video tape deck. I hoped the recording would provide me with materials for study when I returned to my home studios after the residency. The recording is included in this package because it's representative of emergent music that includes set parts, in this case the pre-composed music and the source video that you may recognize from the Hewlett-Packard session. Because nobody was initially at the recording controls, later it was necessary for me to massage, with the help of my Mac, both the audio and the video so the study could be included here.

This piece is typical, not necessarily in style but in process, of what comes together during my university residencies. During the course of an introductory lecture-demonstration, I extend an open invitation to all parties interested in getting involved in the process of collaborating on performances for a public program. In effect, it's an open audition for a show that's already scheduled for a few days down the road. We meet at another scheduled time to hear/see/discuss what the local artists might like to program of their work, and, with their consultation, I weave their personal work into the context of my visual music work and compose a public program or two.

DVD Volume 1
Set Two:
9. SR HP Flight 5

Remember that this session was in Northern California in 1984 and the New Age was on the rise. Hippies never disappeared. They just morphed. The local California State University was at that time still called "Granola U" by many of the local residents. It's sweet, isn't it? Despite what you might suspect, there was absolutely no smoke at the session. Also no participant in the Hewlett-Packard session ever said "let's not go there", so when we found ourselves drifting in a certain direction, that's where we played for a time. Consider how distant in nature Flight 5 is from Flight 4 whereas they were adjacent to each other in time. It's in the nature of self-organizing systems to be more or less unpredictable and therein lies much of their charm. It's similar to being on a search for the connections between love and surrender. (Does that mean anything? Of course it does!)

For more detailed information see Chapter 18, The Hewlett-Packard Session.

DVD Volume 1
Set Two:
10. SR HP Flight 8

The opening image is generated by the video synthesizer and that's followed and joined by the laser animation system producing material that looks oscillographic. Visually what emerges is a classical meditative duet. Midway through the flight, after Paul alters the assignments on his video synthesizer control inputs, the musicians discover they can trigger and otherwise influence the imagery, and the game changes. Look and listen for the changes.

For more detailed information see Chapter 18, The Hewlett-Packard Session.

DVD Volume 1
Set Two:
11. Deb Fox Tour One

The two Deb Fox Tours are from The Deb Fox Heterophonic Alchemical Tours, a visual music video project I started in 2000. I expected it to occupy me for many months because I wanted to record a fully fleshed out example of a showcasing process I explored often over the years on the road, but other projects quickly pushed it to a back burner; so I'm left with bins of materials still waiting for my attention. Like many of my compositions since the late 1960s, this is a targeted study to integrate the latest affordable emerging technology in the electronic arts with the spirit of a specific performance artist. Such studies are my favorite vehicles for learning about the gear as well as learning about the performing artists. Typically I've done such pieces with local artists in a very accelerated form when I'm doing week-long residencies on the road; the performing artists have been dancers, poets, theater folks, and all sorts of musicians. Our collaborations always result in a piece that is programmed on a public event, consequently our focus on the coming performance never seems to allow enough time to conduct a recording process properly, so it's never part of the schedule.

In brief, what happens in the process is that a piece emerges or precipitates from a semi-anticipated evolving cloud of hardware, software, people, ideas, and technical problems. One of the objectives of the process is to sculpt the unpredictable into something that is somewhat more predictable, and eventually presentable to an audience as a game being played by performance artists. The notion of "on-the-fly" is extended from the moment to a longer time scale, anywhere from hours to days. It's hours when there's the pressure to perform publicly as part of a residency and days when the context is more of social gathering. The purpose is more the learning process than it is the finished piece. Most of my set pieces are born of this process; often the pieces that remain in my concert rotation longest (the set pieces) are those that emphatically demonstrate to me something I hadn't imagined initially, in other words, something I learned that was worthy of further study and field testing.

Deb Fox is a San Francisco multi-instrumentalist performance artist. Her history includes performances with numerous bands in San Francisco, Boston, and Hawaii. In late 2000 after we met at an Other Minds event in San Francisco, we scheduled a number of meetings to explore common ground in the arts. Eventually we scheduled a session to record her playing whatever she felt like doing consistent with the idea of integrating realtime composition and her personal stream of consciousness music expression. All the basic unprocessed material found on Deb Fox Tour One, Deb Fox Tour Two, and Deb Fox Additional Video Files is derived from one long recording session at one of my Eastman Lane studios in the hills west of Petaluma.

Heterophony is a term with roots in the philosophy of Plato. It refers to a freely created form of polyphony that simultaneously employs slightly to more considerably modified versions of the same musical structures (usually melody) by two or more performers. (In this case my computer processing counts as the second performer.) Most likely the idea of heterophony emerged close on the heels of melody when people first started making music together, and that certainly was a long time ago, so heterophony has the benefit of a very long tradition. Especially in the music of regular folks, heterophony has always remained paramount. In its simplest form it's just follow the leader as closely as possible; good mistakes (variations) are encouraged as a form of sound spice. What I've always found most seductive about heterophony is that the leading edge of a musical structure seems to cut through the space of time surrounding itself with a wake of its own influences and leaving long trailing, ornamental clouds at the same time.

In the global music of the 21st century heterophony continues to play a fundamental structural role though often involving more recent (past four or five centuries?) intellectual devices such as augmentation, diminution, ornamentation, etc., and at the emerging technological level, adjustable windows on all music variables. Every single tone you hear in the Deb Fox Tours is derived heterophonically from the playing of Deb Fox in one way or another, thanks to MetaSynth, a software synthesizer for the Mac. That's just another way of saying that the spirit of Deb Fox is embedded in the music. Listen for it.

Alchemy in the arts can be viewed as a process for transforming what is mined from an experience and adding value and personal color to it by putting it in the company of other experiences and processes (gardeners: think from compost heap to edible delights). It's a method of combining and tuning multidimensional matrices to create new higher level forms often beyond anticipation—a method that is an ideal environment for exploring, learning, and creating. For The Deb Fox Heterophonic Alchemical Tours, the visual music alchemical tool set is an electronic arts synthesizer made up of the combination of U&I Software products—MetaSynth, MetaTrack, ArtMatic Pro, Videodelic, and Xx. These are software products for the Macintosh computer by Eric Wenger, one of the premiere software designers of the late 20th/early 21st centuries; he was based in San Francisco at the time the work on this piece was done.

The Tours are various paths through a set of emergent music and visual music explorations. The individual pieces are composed to stand alone or to be considered modules that can be placed into various sequences (the tours) according to production requirements. Look for Deb Fox's images in the abstract animations. She's everywhere all the time.

As a composer, especially in my performance-multimedia work on the road, I've collaborated with artists who exhibit a broad range of technical proficiency. From my compositional perspective the technical facility of a performing artist always takes second place to the spiritual honesty, authenticity, and transparency of the artist in performance. My collaborative work is targeted at supporting and showcasing the spirit of my collaborator as it manifests through their work. That approach makes for a great learning environment for all concerned.

DVD Volume 1
Set Two:
12. Deb Fox Tour Two

See the text of Deb Fox Tour One.

SIX

DVD Volume 2

DVD Volume 2
Set One:
1. Elizabeth

Daniel Feiler, an undergraduate at the University of Wisconsin—Madison plays the electric space bass (his terminology) on one of the public events I produced there as part of a week-long residency in 1999. I did the performance-videography; for a detailed description of performance-videography see the last two paragraphs of the notes on Cynthia's Dream.

Only relatively short excerpts are included because this study is based on a recording of a live performance with nobody at the recording controls. One leg of the audio/video, that was distributed to multiple video monitors, a projector, and speakers, was patched into a video tape deck that I hoped would provide me with materials for study when I returned to my studios after the residency. In this case the unattended video deck couldn't handle the levels of his guitar processor collection. It was a wonderful sound live but it didn't translate very well to the recording medium except in bits and pieces.

The source tape for the performance-videography was generated with a software video synthesizer called Bliss Paint. It's the flagship product of software designer Greg Jalbert's company in Berkeley, CA. More examples of Bliss Paint output used as a source tape can be seen on Bliss & Contact Dance and Beyond the Event Horizon; both studies can be found on DVD Volume 2, Set 2.

DVD Volume 2
Set One:
2. SR HP Flight 2

An unusual feature of this flight is the camera play of Diane Kitchell as she's picking up the projected synthesizer-driven laser animations. Most camera folks don't think to move the camera and play its controls. Diane's camera dancing radically alters the visual meaning of the laser animation.

For more detailed information see Chapter 18, The Hewlett-Packard Session.

DVD Volume 2
Set One:
3. SR HP Flight 6

Two excerpts are included from this flight. The first has sound which is slightly distorted because of the nature of the sound plus the fact that the recording deck was unattended. The second excerpt has no sound because the audio circuit was overdriven thus resulting in a sound distorted beyond repair.

The visual material from this flight has been used numerous times as a source tape in my performance-videography events. It opens with one of my favorite laser images. It's a dynamic portal that's electronic in nature but it also has the look of classical oriental calligraphy; plus it leaves colorful cloudy trails in its wake. Especially from viewing the second excerpt, it's easy to see that there's plenty of negative space in the video and that makes it well suited for combining with live camera work that slips imagery into that space. Cynthia's Dream is a good study for getting a sense of how this imagery can be combined with that of a live camera.

For more detailed information see Chapter 18, The Hewlett-Packard Session.

DVD Volume 2
Set One:
4. SR HP Flight 3

Once more, Diane's play with the movement of the camera and with its controls transforms the laser animations.

Some of the local poppers can be heard joining the mainstay musicians in this recording. As can be heard from the stylistic range of music in the flights, the band of musicians was in flux all session long.

For more detailed information see Chapter 18, The Hewlett-Packard Session.

DVD Volume 2
Set One:
5. SR HP Flight 1

This is an excerpt from the beginning of the session. We were playing in the test mode. No audio is included here because the audio circuits were overdriven, thus the recording was distorted.

The flights, 1 - 8, are labeled in chronological order although that is not how they appear on DVDs. To get a sense of how the group gelled over the course of the session, it would be instructive to compare flights at various points in the timeline of the session. The flight number indicates where they fall in the time progression of the session.

For more detailed information see Chapter 18, The Hewlett-Packard Session.

DVD Volume 2
Set Two:
6. Bliss & Contact Dance

This is an excerpt from a performance of Dijucontact, a piece programmed on one of the concerts I produced in 1999 at the conclusion of a residency at the University of Wisconsin—Madison. The dancers are UW undergraduates Mary Darcy, Janine Jones, and AJ Niehaus. The musician on dijiradu is Kevin Frey, a doctoral candidate in music. I did the performance videography. Sad to say because it was done so beautifully in live performance, there is no audio on this recording. Even if we had planned a recording session for this piece, it would have been very difficult to capture the sound with a sufficient degree of fidelity because Kevin Frey was often on the move interacting with the dancers.

To do the performance-videography I was working with a visual music configuration I'd been developing since the late 1980s, so I'd been exploring its possibilities for over a decade before this performance. The way it works is that in realtime I capture the action of the performers on stage with an analog video camera on my right shoulder, while my left hand is playing an Amiga 1000 which is simultaneously digitizing and processing the video image stream generated by the camera. A Super Gen is used to mix the Amiga output of that stream with a source tape of video imagery which in this performance was produced with software called Bliss Paint. The output of the Super Gen, which is the final video stream mix, is sent out to multiple video monitors and projection systems that surround the performers on stage. Consequently the audience is witnessing the dance, the musicians, the video performance, and the multiple video monitors and projection systems simultaneously.

Occasionally when the conditions permit, as they did in this instance, I split the video stream and send one leg out to a video recorder so I can study the action later at my leisure. It's important to note that viewing all these excerpts is like seeing the action through my camera's viewfinder. Unlike being at the performance where it's possible to see many actions simultaneously and to change your point of view at will, looking through my viewfinder has, by its inherent limitations, a very restricted field of view, and moreover what what you see is not under your control.

Nevertheless, the upside is that, since I have considerable experience with this process, what you see through my viewfinder is certainly worth studying as an experienced point of view. But personally I would always prefer to be free to look at whatever I desire, and to make a viewing adjustment whenever I choose. The way to achieve those ends is to both attend to and do live performances; because you are free to perceive as you prefer, the live performances are always more exciting than recordings, plus they also sound and look so much richer because the information makes it to your ears and eyes without being limited or distorted by intervening electromechanical translation (recording) systems.

The source tape for Dijucontact was generated with Bliss Paint, a truly unique animation tool that's the brainchild of Greg Jalbert, a San Francisco Bay Area artist who has produced a variety of useful tools for those who practice the electronic arts of sound and light. In keeping with Jalbert's general outlook on life, what he makes available in Bliss Paint seems to grow naturally out of what's possible to do with the Macintosh computer. The geometry, the movement, and the colors just seem to flow easily out of the heart of the computer—no mean feat when you consider all the clumsiness computers seem to engender.

Jalbert's software shows an unusual level of respect for what the Macintosh represents (the collaboration of some of the most creative minds in the computer industry) when he seems to ask of it a simple question—Well, my friend, what exactly is it that you can do on a fundamental level with light as a dynamical system? The answers are collected by Greg into a huge library of animated shapes and patterns that interact with his dynamic color tools. In an absolutely true sense Bliss Paint turns the Macintosh into a powerful video synthesizer that has a built-in sequencer into which all the light tools can be plugged in ways that sculpt the flow of time. Plus the system can be controlled by MIDI and sound input, and the visual output can be projected live or recorded to any video medium. While you are composing the sequence of events, the visual feedback on what's being created is instantaneous; so working with this software usually puts the player in a higher state of mind—when you close down your session, a text message appears on the screen informing you of how long you've been Blissed out ;-)

DVD Volume 2
Set Two:
7. UW Rockers

This an excerpt from a performance by an undergraduate art rock group at the University of Wisconsin—Madison, a group that was included on one of the public events I produced there as part of a week-long residency in 1999. The group is known as "fore": Ryan Corcoran, guitar and vocals; Luke Skoug, bass; and Josh Pierce, drums. I did the performance-videography; for a detailed description of performance-videography see the last two paragraphs of the notes on Cynthia's Dream.

It's rare for one of my university public events not to include a rock group. With good reason they're drawn to the opportunity to be featured in the context of a live stage version of music video. And they always get strong positive feedback from the audience. Look at these guys—they are having the time of their lives, and we're just viewing it through a tiny portal. On stage, it's big. And yes, grandma, it was both good and **LOUD**—and that's after, in accordance with my bidding, they potted it down to make the levels work in the concert hall. Sorry, no audio on this recording; the unattended deck choked on it.

Notice Ryan playing/dancing to and off the projected video of his computer-processed image. Some people pick up on the feedback play very quickly and work it to everyone's advantage—he was one of those people.

DVD Volume 2
Set Two:
8. SR HP Flight 7

This is a very simple pas de deux involving two electronic visual music instruments—the video synthesizer and the synthesizer driven laser animation system. I doubt the sexual overtones require explanation. It's hypnotic quality makes it a good fit as a source tape for especially lyrical performers.

For more detailed information see Chapter 18, The Hewlett-Packard Session.

DVD Volume 2
Set Two:
9. Beyond The Event Horizon

This study is one of many different collections of visual materials that I use as source tapes to be mixed with the imagery picked up live by a video camera in my pieces that call for performance-videography. Source material such as this is usually created in a studio setting, and then stored on a playback medium such as videotape, DVD, or a hard drive. More rarely I'll use as source material imagery that was recorded in a previous performance or exploratory gathering. Over the years I've put together a large collection of sources; just before I'm off to gig, I select whatever I anticipate might be most appropriate for the nature of the engagement.

If the gig is a residency at a university, I wait until after the audition process before I even think about making a decision on which source tape to use for a particular performance. Some of the variables to consider are: how many performers will there be, what will they be doing, what is the character of the piece, what's the duration of the piece, what computer configuration will I be using with the camera imagery, etc. When it seems appropriate I treat the choice of source material as another collaborative variable; so there are times when, after showing performers some possibilities, I ask them for their preferences.

To make it easier to remember and to access the sources I give them what I think of as descriptive titles. Regarding this particular source, including event horizon in the title makes it very easy to remember what it contains. In theoretical physics the event horizon is defined as the area surrounding a black hole. A black hole is so dense that nothing can escape its gravitational field within a certain boundary and that boundary is the event horizon. So theoretically, light (and maybe time) is drawn into the hole but more recently there are some theorists who believe that some radiation manages to escape the pull of the black hole. Therefore, the visual material of this source mostly seems to be drawn into the hole, but occasionally some of it seems to be escaping it at the same time. Whenever I see the title, I see the material; so as a mnemonic device it works perfectly well.

The imagery was created with Bliss Paint. See the description of that software in the Bliss & Contact Dance notes.

DVD Volume 2
Set Two:
10. Deb Fox Additional Video Files

This is an example of a file collection from which material can be selected for composing a source tape to be used in performance-videography. It can also be considered as a bin for storing the experiments of a particular subject that is processed by a particular software application. The first step in the process of creating file collections is capturing a performer or an event with a video camera. Then what's captured is used as an input to a computer running software that can transform that imagery in a variety of ways. In this case I'm working with Eric Wenger's ArtMatic software which functions as a video synthesizer based on principles derived from Chaos Theory.

The ArtMatic user experiments with configuring flowcharts composed of sets of selectable operations that transform the video image in a variety of ways with amazingly fast feedback. The game is to experiment with flowcharts and their outputs until something emerges that captures your fancy. Included in that experimentation, once you've been properly seduced by a flowchart, are fine-tuning variables to coax the system to give you what you'd prefer most. As with any other synthesizer you work to discover how operations play with and off each other; then you can adjust the variables to create an outcome that is closer to what might meet your inclinations and preferences. What often happens is that you don't discover that you need something until after you've made it; the need seems to emerge along with the material.

It's important to remember when you're creating collections that not every file is meant to stand alone. You'll need material that works as background, middle ground, and foreground as well as in the solo, contrapuntal, and support modes. For example, material that's slow, dark or has considerable negative space works well as background whereas action-filled material that articulates the entire space works well as foreground. In the middle of the process, well before you should actually commit yourself to a final version, a good procedure is to experiment with as many variations as possible, all the while imagining various application scenarios. Think of this part of the process as the fun part; it's protocompositional. Don't cheat yourself out of it, because this is when most of the learning happens and when a piece begins to suggest and assume various shapes.

For more detailed information see the notes for Deb Fox Tour One.

DVD Volume 2
Set Two:
11. Musings Collection One

This is an example of a file collection that focuses on a particular notion, in this case, videographic fluid dynamics, for generation of which ArtMatic is especially well suited.

Often in the midst of free play, material emerges that stops you in your tracks and forces you to consider it as a theme that requires multiple variations. That's no time to be an ingrate; instead be friendly and show your gratitude by playing its possibilities and collecting your favorites as you go.

For related information see the notes on the Deb Fox Additional Video Files entry.

SEVEN

DVD Volume 3:
Pythagoras & Pellegrino
In Petaluma

DVD Volume 3
Sample Suite

Sample Suite is composed of excerpts from all 10 studies included on DVD Volumes 3 and 4. It runs for about 22 minutes. It's intended to provide an overview of all the studies as well as to function as a concert piece.

For more detailed information see the chapters (20 - 24) in the section on Pythagoras & Pellegrino In Petaluma.

DVD Volume 3
Study 1 - Kate

Named after the oldest of my granddaughters.

The motion is generated by phase changes caused by very slight to more exaggerated detunings from the exact integer multiples in the ratios. As the ratios approach from either direction the exact integer multiples, the movement gradually slows, until it completely stops when it reaches an exact integer multiple. Use headphones or listen in the stereo sweet spot and you'll hear sonic motion that corresponds to the visual motion.

The more complex the waveforms, the more complex the image, the more complex the timbre. Sense and follow the evolution of the complexity.

Watch for the visual artifacts that result from the beating of the video capture rate against the frequencies used to drive the galvanometers.

For more detailed information see the chapters (20 - 24) in the section on Pythagoras & Pellegrino In Petaluma.

DVD Volume 3
Study 2 - Lia

Named after my youngest granddaughter.

The opening look is oscillographic which for me is like having a conversation with an old friend. The story of the relationship between the two fundamental waves unfolds very slowly and is clearly written out in sound and light.

The small waves (higher frequencies) superimposed on the crests and troughs of the larger waves (lower frequencies) are a combination of spectral components and nonlinear signatures—spectral components of the x and y signals and the resonant frequencies of the galvanometers.

For more detailed information see the chapters (20 - 24) in the section on Pythagoras & Pellegrino In Petaluma.

DVD Volume 3
Study 3 - Ray

Named after Ray Charles. How he always manages to sing such highly complex sounds (composed of multiphonics with huge spectral spreads) heavy with feeling and perfectly in tune never ceases to amaze me. We can only celebrate his genius.

This is a study of spectral play accessed by way of playing a resonating low-pass filter.

For more detailed information see the chapters (20 - 24) in the section on Pythagoras & Pellegrino In Petaluma.

DVD Volume 3
Study 4 - Yo-Yo

The sounds of Yo-Yo Ma playing his cello have been a companion of mine for a long time; especially loved is his work with J.S. Bach's 6 Unaccompanied Cello Suites.

For more detailed information see the chapters (20 - 24) in the section on Pythagoras & Pellegrino In Petaluma.

EIGHT

DVD Volume 4: Pythagoras & Pellegrino In Petaluma

DVD Volume 4
Study 5 - Malie

Named after a granddaughter who, in a recent chess match, rallied from near defeat to corner me for checkmate. That was one of those rare situations when you could be both humbled and proud.

This piece pushes the limits of video's capability to capture laser animations with any degree of fidelity. The higher the frequency, the faster the movement of the laser beam. The faster the movement of the laser beam, the less light there is to be captured by the video recording system.

It's also worth noting that the higher the fundamental frequencies, the more difficult it is to control the movement in the images. Bear in mind that the manual control for frequency is a knurled knob on a 5-turn potentiometer. Very slight rotations of the knob will generate a tuning difference that creates the phase differences that cause movement in the images; it gets to the point where in order for the movement to be slight enough you have to lean on the knob with your thought.

For more detailed information see the chapters (20 - 24) in the section on Pythagoras & Pellegrino In Petaluma.

DVD Volume 4
Study 6 - Keb

Named after Keb' Mo', sweetest blues player around. Always good to hear him again and his singing was in the air the day this piece was being polished.

For more detailed information see the chapters (20 - 24) in the section on Pythagoras & Pellegrino In Petaluma.

DVD Volume 4
Study 7 - WAG

WAG are the initials for my grandson, William Allen Guy.

This is an extended study that explores low frequency phase relationships used to generate rhythmic patterns in counterpoint with florid higher frequencies that spin out visual melodies that ease in and out of the virtual space for periods of various lengths.

For more detailed information see the chapters (20 - 24) in the section on *Pythagoras & Pellegrino In Petaluma*.

DVD Volume 4
Study 8 - Nella

Nella is my mother's nickname.

This is one of my favorite old-time laser ragas. It works especially well in large spaces with white walls. Imagine this imagery filling a forward reflective wall and occasionally stretching upwards to crawl along the ceiling. For this DVD I made an effort to keep it in the monitor box, but it obviously wants out. Some forms of lyrical can be also be dramatic.

For more detailed information see the chapters (20 - 24) in the section on Pythagoras & Pellegrino In Petaluma.

DVD Volume 4
Study 9 - Astor

Astor Piazzolla—composer of tango music that plays your heart. His music was in the air around the time I was polishing this piece.

For more detailed information see the chapters (20 - 24) in the section on Pythagoras & Pellegrino In Petaluma.

DVD Volume 4
Study 10 - Meg

Named after a granddaughter with a fiery spirit.

Often when I'm working in my studio, alone or with a guest, this laser raga works as a powerful cyberspirit attractor. Unfortunately the attraction seems mostly lost in video and computer translations, but there's a chance some of you might sense it; or it could be that my memories of those studio experiences are just playing on my perception. For more information on cyberspirits, see the essay on Compositional Algorithms as Cyberspirit Attractors in the Compositional Theory section.

For more detailed information see the chapters (20 - 24) in the section on Pythagoras & Pellegrino In Petaluma.

Glossary

aesthetics of music: the philosophical study of musical values.

alchemy in the arts: a process for transforming what is mined from an experience and adding value and personal color to it by putting it in the company of other experiences and processes.

algorithms in the arts: systems that make their way through interactive relationships or a sequence of computer instructions that result in states that attract the attention of artists because they feel, look, or sound like art processes or products.

ArtMatic: software by Eric Wenger that gives the user access to dynamical systems algorithms represented in the user interface as a set of selectable flowcharts composed of selectable mathematical functions. The software is beautifully designed to encourage the user to experiment with complex dynamical systems at multiple levels (structures, functions, and parameters) and gives one almost instant visual feedback on what happens when the algorithms are modified, the functions are rearranged, and/or parameters are fine-tuned.

authentic: expression uniquely emerging from an individual's history and perspective.

complexity theory: an approach to analyzing or studying systems that are too complex to predict their outcomes with much accuracy, yet still show underlying patterns that make certain outcomes more or less probable.

compositional algorithm: a more or less complex system composed of a pliable network that includes: 1. generative and control functions, 2. internal and external influences, modifiers, and drivers, and 3. feedback loops, all working together in an integrated and interactive process to create a dynamical structure with lifelike properties. The lifelike properties include macrostructural predictability and reliability built upon a substructure characterized by ebb and flow around equilibrium points, variable windows on indeterminacy, and controllable volatility.

compositional field-tests: exercised opportunities for putting your work in front of people and being there in person to make compositional adjustments so as to get a clearer sense of just what, how much, and how well your material communicates to them.

creativity software: algorithms and generative systems that make it relatively easy for the any user to produce the illusion of a work of art.

cyberspirits: presences that more or less inhabit the processes of technological systems depending upon the consciousness levels of the original creators of the technology in combination with the attitudes of the users of the technology; ephemeral forms that seem to emerge from the ether to join in play and to offer suggestions on directions to explore; sometimes they assume their ephemeral forms by emerging from the very natures of the sound and light instruments and tools, whether they are hardware or software.

dynamic equilibrium: (in the creation of laser animations) expressed as the nature of the movement to, from, and around the intersections of the whole number ratios.

dynamical forms: moving and changing; forms created by periodic patterns, their intersections, and their interactions.

electronic arts of sound and light: a field based on the idea of using emerging technology to create sound and light forms that inform, extend, challenge, and delight the senses.

emergent music: difficult to predict music that grows out of algorithms or systems with environments designed or naturally configured to promote self-organization. The composer's role is to create or to find algorithms or systems that are appropriate for this function, as well as to make aesthetic judgments on the musical value of what emerges from those algorithms and systems. Furthermore, it is the composer's role to fine-tune the configuration's variables so as to emphasize what is deemed most desirable as output features.

entrainment: the tendency for two oscillating systems in close proximity to lock into phase so they vibrate in synchrony; somehow the systems seem to exhibit mutual influence. Entrainment is a universal principle that operates across the spectrum of life.

envelope: the onset, development, and decay of waveform variables over time.

ephemeral forms: forms passing so quickly they hardly seem to exist. Just how long they seem to exist depends upon time scales.

event: a collection of fields joined by coincidental properties serving to create and reinforce an identity.

Fairlight Voicetracker: a special purpose computer for analyzing and converting audio frequency, amplitude, waveshape, and duration to MIDI signals.

feedback: a process that involves some part of a system's output being returned to it's input.

frequency: cycles per unit of time. In music, pitch refers to the frequency of a waveform, the number of times it cycles per second.

galvanometers: (for laser deflection) small motors that translate the electronic wavetrains of a synthesizer to mechanical vibrations that drive the small posts on the galvanometers to which very light-weight mirrors are affixed.

generic composition: integrating parts and elements into a whole.

graphic scores: music scores that create their own symbolic notation that visually or graphically suggest time-based gestures, frequency curves, articulation regimes, and whatever else is deemed appropriate for the context. In effect graphic scores are symbolic invitations to performing musicians to participate in the compositional process.

heterophony: a freely created form of polyphony that simultaneously employs slightly to more considerably modified versions of a lead musical structure (usually melody) by two or more performers.

laser animation: imagery created by a point of laser light moving fast enough to leave a trail in your visual perception. The laser images are drawn out over time by a deflected point of laser light following paths prescribed by the interaction of the audio stereo wavetrains driving mirrors via their galvanometers.

limen: a just noticeable difference, the threshold of a physiological or psychological response.

Lissajous figures: images formed by creating curves in one plane traced by a point moving under the influence of two separate harmonic motions.

matrix: Mathematics: A rectangular array of numeric or algebraic quantities subject to mathematical operations. Computer Science: The network of intersections between input and output leads in a computer.

matrix alignment: analysis that clarifies the nature and the meaning formed by the intersections of one or more multidimensional matrices.

Metaesthetics List: an international online group of tech artists that collaborated in the exploration, development, and articulation of metatheories of the electronic arts of sound and light that include an integrative approach to music, dynamic visual art, established technology, emerging technology, cybernetics, metaphysics, psychophysics, psychology, mathematics, sociology, communications theory, ancient knowledge, emerging knowledge, and other related branches of human learning and searching.

metatheory: a theory of another theory or set of theories.

module: a self-contained part of a system. In music synthesizers, it's a part that operates on waveform variables—frequency, amplitude, spectra, and phase.

morphology: in the arts, the study of form and content especially as they relate to perceptual and emotional impact.

multidimensional matrix: a mathematical table that has more than two dimensions.

multimedia: a presentation form that employs multiple media vehicles such as music, video, dance, film, theater lighting, and laser projections.

music: a natural or invented dynamical (moving and changing) system perceived as trails of sonic patterns pregnant with subcultural, cultural, and archetypal symbolism endowed with the power to affect the soul

mystic: one who seeks the truth by going beyond sensory information and beyond rational thought, though both might function as springboards.

omnimedia: performance-multimedia based on applying emerging technology in the arts as the magnet for attracting all manner of other art media for public performance.

open art system: an integrative way of thinking that seeks harmony with anyone in the arts, any media, any venue, and any context.

oscillographic images: images generated by an oscilloscope, a piece of electronic gear that visually represents the voltages at its inputs.

perception: the process of grasping the meaning of sensory information as it filters through and is shaped by the memories of past experiences and cultural biases.

performance field tests: concerts and other public presentations for the purpose of testing experimental art materials.

performance-multimedia: realtime performance of multimedia.

performance-videography: realtime video capturing, digitizing, and processing of musicians, dancers or other performance artists, and then mixing those video streams on-the-fly with pre-composed video animations (source tapes).

periodic systems: vibrations recurring at regular intervals of time.

persistence of vision: a psycho-optical phenomenon characteristic of the human visual system that results in sustaining an image for a short time after its cause is removed.

poetics of dynamics: the art of articulating and moving through time.

protocompositional: the gestation stages of composition, the period when the first ideas begin to precipitate from an amorphous cloud of the partly-formed.

psychophysics: a field devoted to the physical nature of sensory stimuli, the nature of human perception and responses to those stimuli, and the cultural influences on perception.

Pythagoras of Samos: a mystical, mathematical, and acoustical philosopher, who along with his followers in the 6th century BC and beyond, set the stage for the development of psychophysics (the physics of the senses) in the present day.

ragas and talas: (for laser animations) performable collections of visual melodies, scales, tunings, shapes, ornaments, and rhythms to be used in a realtime compositional mode.

realtime composition: an exercise in composition that relies on the principle of "tuning on-the-fly," that is, making adjustments to compositional variables according to the requirements of the moment.

resonance: a dynamic state of being that occurs in a system when it is excited by an external stimulus with coincidental wave characteristics.

significant forms: those that embody or reflect authentic feelings or perspectives that communicate to, connect with, and grow out of the fundamental human drive to promote the evolution of the senses and the higher levels of consciousness.

sonification: the use of non-speech sound for modeling, exploring, and conveying information in the arts and science.

source tapes: pre-composed video animations or video recordings of other events intended to be mixed on-the-fly with realtime video capturing, digitizing, and processing of musicians, dancers or other performance artists.

spectral component: one of the frequencies, called a partial, from the mix of frequencies that gives sound its tone color or timbre. The partials (spectral components) can be harmonically related to the fundamental (whole number ratios) or inharmonically related (non-integer ratios).

sweet spot: in the stereo audio field, a spot found near the apex of an equilateral triangle formed by you and the stereo speakers.

systems: sets of internally related parts.

Taoist magic forms: the talismans of unorthodox Chinese calligraphic expression that are used to invoke the blessings of the spirits.

The Real* Electric Symphony: a variable group of sound, light, and movement performance artists engaged in public performances based on a realtime compositional process born of a conversational approach to creating performance art, an approach that encourages the participants to bring to bear whatever they wanted to offer of their history as well as their insight into the moment.

transient: an aspect of an event that has a short duration. In sound it normally refers to the attack (onset) although it can also refer to other short-lived spectral phenomena as the event unfolds.

variable: a function whose value is subject to change.

virtual reality: normally thought of as a computer simulated environment, although composers historically have referred to virtual aspects of their music particularly the virtual space of voicing and orchestration as well as the sonic images that fill performance venues.

visual music: an integrated multimedia approach to music based on the principle that there are both natural visual manifestations and invented visual representations, connections, reflections, translations, mappings, and embodiments of all sonic musical elements, structures, and processes.

waveform variables: frequency, amplitude, phase, and spectral components.

Ylem: an art and technology community that meets often for information exchanges in San Francisco at the Exploratorium, San Francisco Bay Area Universities, and other art, science, and cultural spaces.

Acknowledgments

As I write the final section of this book, it feels like I'm composing a Thanksgiving prayer. Writing this is a wonderful ego-busting exercise because it helps one to realize that there's a world of people, institutions, events, and environments living in you and through you. Some demons too. Modern molecular biology tells us that long-term memory is maintained through special self-perpetuating proteins; these special proteins are located at synaptic terminals newly grown when produced by sensations that are repeated, shocking or inspirational. What that means is that all we remember is actually a material translation of our significant experiences, whatever their causes, and that we literally carry them—the experiences via the proteins—with us throughout our lives. And it's not like they're dead weight; they're living at our synaptic terminals which means they occupy key positions not only in our brains but also where the associated sensory and motor neurons communicate.

Many of those proteins are programs barking out marching orders. In fact, those programs are competing proteins battling each other for supremacy over influencing us in how we conduct our lives. Thus the notion of demons is not just a metaphor—they truly are our constant companions in the form of undesirable programs folded into self-perpetuating proteins in long-term residence at our most critical neural junctions. The upshot is that there's a boisterous crowd living in every one of us. Living freely as an I is neither easy nor simple because every member of the onboard mob behaves as if its destiny is to take the lead and show us the one true way. So if much of our lives must be consumed by dancing with and around our battling programs, the best we can do is to focus on those that influence us in ways the we and our fellow six-and-half billion travelers find more, rather than less desirable. Let the good influences reign and roll.

My greatest debt is to my father, called Aurelio as a child in Italy and then Ernest after he left Ellis Island on his way to the American Midwest as 12 year old immigrant. I knew him as a family man working two jobs to provide for a family of six children and a live-in mother-in-law. I expect my love of realtime is directly connected with certain admonitions delivered by him when we were together in his car as he ferried me to music rehearsals or athletic practices on his way to his second job. From my preteen years on through high school I was told by him many times in many ways that it was important to figure out how to design a life that avoided the obligation of "punching a time-clock." Sometimes I think I was so thoroughly programmed along those lines that some of my DNA switches were flipped to and locked down to the free mode. I have no regret, only gratitude for those talks, especially because I was fortunate enough to be born in the land of the free. Eventually I came to interpret "time-clock" as a metaphor for any system, social or mechanical, not of my own free choice. Exercising that freedom of choice eventually became my main form of being, always of course in harmony with the prevailing conditions which, fortunately, most often are also subject to choice.

I'm indebted to my parents for encouraging my musical impulses from my earliest years. My memories take me back to my time in the crib when I was hearing arias from Italian operas coming out of our Victrola in the living room. So it's no surprise that my musical tendencies emphasize melodies. While still in Italy my mother's father made his living by composing, conducting, and playing the trumpet in various opera houses around Italy. Consequently my mother, Nella, grew up enveloped by those arias floating in her air and they followed her into our home. During the early 1940s the sounds of arias coming off 78s often filled our family space, with the voice of Enrico Caruso, one of my mother's favorites, dominating the air waves.

I'm indebted to the musicians and the institutions supportive of music in my birthplace, Kenosha, Wisconsin, a small industrial town (during my years there) on Lake Michigan midway between Chicago and Milwaukee. In my youth it was populated by many immigrants from Italy, Germany, Russia, and Poland and among them were musicians who played on the local scene. Art Peck, first chair clarinetist with the Kenosha Civic Band, sold my parents a very old tarnished metal clarinet for my use, an instrument that I personally found was particularly good at squeaking, That's the instrument that got me started when I was nine years old and I'm forever grateful to Mr. Peck for passing it along to me and also giving me my first music lesson one memorable evening in our kitchen on 54th Street. Not so long afterwards I managed to get a "first" clarinet—at least that's what I told Mr. Dolittle, my grade school's music teacher, because my new clarinet was actually made of wood!

A few years later I had the privilege of sitting behind Mr. Peck in the Civic Band after my brother Ernie Jr., a trumpeter, and I were invited to join the band when we were still in our early teens (our private teacher, Frank Nicolai, conducted the band). The first rehearsal provided spine-tingling thrills I'll never forget. There we were, a couple of kids in a band otherwise entirely populated by adults who were adept at playing transcriptions of European orchestra and opera music as well as marches from all the greats, including Sousa and his cohorts That was a band that, during the summer months, with one hour of rehearsal a week would present several weekly concerts of an hour-and-a-half—my capacity for sight-reading was, by necessity, greatly enhanced during my years with that band.

Kenosha was also blessed with a very active Catholic Youth Organization band; we presented concerts and marched in parades in all the major cities of the Midwest including Detroit, Chicago, Cleveland, and Milwaukee. During the 1950s the Mary D. Bradford High School music scene was especially vibrant because of a then recently hired energetic city-wide music supervisor, Ralph Houghton—we had concert and marching bands, an orchestra, choirs, and a stage band led by a senior student (I was fortunate enough to play that role). The stage band in those days played mostly big band swing arrangements by the greats from the 1940s and 1950s; it also organized variety shows that ran every spring for several nights. They were always major events attended by folks from every segment of the city.

During the 1950s the Kenosha educational system behaved as though it believed it was in the best interest of its students to explore as much of life as possible. So those of us who were musicians were actually encouraged, rather than discouraged as they are today, from being athletes. From the time I was in grade school there was no question that music was my field for life, but when I was in my youth I wanted to play football, basketball, and run track too. I was able to do that because Kenosha practiced the principles of a liberal arts education, even though they might not have called it that. It is currently our culture's great loss that music and art in early 21st century education have been curtailed and devalued; they have suffered enormously because modern educators have been programmed to turn our youngsters into performance and economic specialists from an early age in keeping with the materialistic tenor of the times.

During my youth in Kenosha I benefited greatly from a strong musician's union, The American Federation of Musicians, that fostered the development of young musicians, including myself by connecting me with paying gigs both as a sideman with other bands and as a leader of my own bands. The union office was located just across the park from the high school so I often dropped in to chat with Frank Zabukovic, the friendly and helpful union agent who connected me with all manner of gigs from sophisticated touring acts to biker's bars across the Illinois state line where we played behind wire-mesh screens to avoid being bopped by flying bottles.

The union also went out of its way to connect young musicians with local adult musicians who were doing special things for the community. One of my favorite people was Manny Mitka, a drummer with considerable gigging experience in major Midwest cities, who set up music stores that functioned as magnets for Kenosha's young musicians. His various stores were always located downtown, so many of us would just drop in when we were near his store and hang out for a while. It was not uncommon to find Manny with one or another of his percussion students drumming out some clever complicated patterns while trading twos, fours, and eights with them. The people I hired for my gigging bands when I was in high school were mostly regulars at Manny Mitka's Music Store.

I would be derelict if I neglected to give due credit to the City of Kenosha and the County of Kenosha for their policy during the 1950s of giving summer day jobs to their young folks, especially during their college years. My jobs with them ranged from playground instructor to running a pneumatic hammer, patching holes and cracks in pavement, and driving a truck on a road crew; those accumulated paychecks went a long way toward covering college expenses. I was just one of many fortunate young people benefiting from those programs; it was a good time to be a kid in Kenosha.

I'm indebted to the Lawrence Conservatory of Music for my early years in formal composition studies with James Ming, a composer on their faculty who spent his summers attending the seminars of Nadia Boulanger in Paris; for four years of undergraduate scholarship support; and for their faculty's encouragement to their students to engage in exploring the full range of musical expression. Ming's approach to teaching composition was perfect for me; it allowed for considerable freedom to explore the content of my daydreams. There wasn't a formal jazz program at that time but the Lawrence faculty and administration supported us jazzers by giving us access to all the available instruments and rehearsal/performance spaces. Lawrence University truly practiced the liberal arts approach to education and it was a perfect fit for someone like me who needed the time, environment, classical instruction, and guidance to make the transition from teenager to young adult. I'm deeply grateful for their patience.

I'm indebted to the University of Wisconsin—Madison for the opportunity to study with master musicians such as Rudolf Kolisch, student of Arnold Schoenberg; René Leibowitz, student of Ravel and Webern; and Robert Crane, student of Howard Hanson. The university rewarded my efforts with various fellowships including a Vilas Fellowship and a Ford Foundation Dissertation Year Fellowship which gave me the first year of freedom in my life, freedom to conduct electronic arts research, to compose, and to record those experiences in the form of a dissertation. That dissertation year set the tone for the rest of my life—do research in the electronic arts, compose, perform, and write.

I'm also indebted to Dr. Harold Luce, a musician whose administrative talents influenced me to take teaching positions at The Ohio State University and Texas Tech University when he chaired those music departments. Harold was unfailingly supportive of any project I presented to him; the list included building electronic arts facilities, publishing a book, traveling for research and events, breaking new ground in music education, and finding seed money for establishing programs to attract outside funding to support the presentation of leading national experimental music performers and composers in local workshops and concerts.

My years with the faculty of Oberlin College Conservatory of Music (1970-75) were ideal in so many ways. At that time, via the New Directions Concert Series, there was a perfectly paced flow of experimental music composers of from five to seven individuals a year visiting the campus. That program provided sufficient inspirational juice to keep everyone at a high energy level for the entire year. Add to that a large collection of highly intelligent, talented, and motivated faculty and students, and the result was a pot that never stopped boiling.

During my time at Oberlin I directed the electronic music studios, a set of four spaces, with administrative support from department chair, to dean, to president of the college, that was a dream-come-true. Oberlin College supported a long research and performance tour I made in Europe to the centers of experimental music activity. It supported a number of trips to San Francisco to do video research at The National Center for Experiments in Television and Project Artaud, an artist's collective. It awarded me a generous research grant to produce the five films of my Lissajous Lives Film Series. Oberlin was wonderful, but it wasn't the San Francisco Bay Area, the only place I've ever found that feels like home to me—it could be that, to feel at home, my Italian genes insist on a combination of a vibrant experimental electronic arts scene, a rich multicultural setting, and, most of all, a Mediterranean climate.

The experiences upon which this book and the DVDs are based simply would not have occurred without the collaboration of numerous artists over the decades, and although all may not be listed here, with gratitude I count them all as my teachers. Every idea in this package required for its realization a society of experimental artists open to taking a fair degree of risk. Thus this package is not based on the work of just one person. By necessity the following lists are highly abbreviated and I extend my apologies to the hundreds of former collaborators not listed here. **Composers/performers:** Salvatore Martirano, Edwin London, Cynthia Fanning, Joan Tower, Joseph Koykkar, John Russell, Pauline Oliveros, Deb Fox, Frankie Mann, Jocy de Oliveira, Gordon Mumma, Herbert Brün, Olly Wilson, Jerry Hunt, James Gillerman, Joseph Celli, Will Johnson, and Charles Moselle. **Filmmakers/ video, photography, and light artists:** Toby Raetze, Phill Niblock, Valrie Hildreth, Diane Kitchell, William Roarty, Willard Rosenquist, Brice Howard, and Robert Pacelli. **Dancers/Choreographers:** Dena Madole, Lynn Dally, Margaret Fisher, Margaret Jenkens, Brenda Way, and Jean Kerr. **Clarinetists:** Lawrence McDonald, Phil Rehfeldt, and David Breeden.

The connections I made with various corporations over the years were absolutely crucial to my research, composition, performance, and theoretical work in the electronic arts. Not much is possible in this field without access to special instruments as well as to exchanges with focused creative thinkers. When I was a new hire at Oberlin in 1970 working to flesh out their studios, Tektronix Inc. came across with one of their top oscilloscopes which became the instrument at the heart of my Lissajous Lives Film Series. A few years later General Scanning Inc. presented me with several sets of audio responsive galvanometers for xyz laser deflection, enough for one system to become a permanent part of the Oberlin studio peripherals and another that's been serving me for the past 34 years. Around the same time, I worked with Buchla Associates on one of the early hybrid systems for audio synthesis, commissioned by California Institute of the Arts. Also during the same period (the mid 1970s) Everett Hafner of EMS of Amherst presented me with two Synthi AKS synthesizers to complete the design of the road system I used for many years.

During the late 1970s I had a consultant gig with Texas Instruments as they were making an effort to enter the microcomputer field. During the early 1980s I was a consultant to alphaSyntauri Inc. in exchange for one of their instruments that set the stage for the MIDI revolution in 1983. In the late 1980s, in exchange for equipment and a percentage of the gross, I contracted to work with Euphonics International Ltd on the design of a hardware/ software system for integrating music and the visual arts via MIDI. In 1989 the Office of the Provost of the California State University system commissioned me to lead a week-long seminar for the CSU Music Department Chairs on the subject of teaching music theory with emerging digital tools for music visualization and synthesis. And in 1994 I was commissioned by the Marketing Department of Fair Isaac Inc., the company that has the final say on our personal creditworthiness, to design and implement one of the first corporate CD-ROM (DVD) facilities that incorporated all phases of production; instructing their staff in its use was also part of the charge. I always found working with the corporate world refreshingly efficient, probably because of their tendency to be extra focused on productivity. There are some good things to be said for the sort of discipline required when attending to the bottom line.

Finally, I'm indebted to various agencies of the United States Government. The National Endowment for the Humanities supported my early research in experimental film and video. The National Endowment for the Arts had a hand in supporting many of my performances over the years and played a crucial role in making one of my projects, The Leading Edge Music Series, happen during the late 1970s and early 1980s at Texas Tech University.

The U.S. State Department sponsored one of my groups, the Real* Electric Symphony, in a European concert tour that led to one of the most memorable times of my life—meeting Ivan Alexandrovich Wyschnegradsky, a Russian expatriate living in Paris, and having him play with us at one of our gigs there. Ivan, a mystic and student of Scriabin, was a bright, energetic 84 years old at the time. He invited several of us to lunch with him at his apartment in Paris where he demonstrated his quarter-tone piano and showed us, among other things, a beautiful book he wrote on the subject of visual music. All of us in the arts need to bow our heads to those inspirational artists who play to the very end, people like Ivan Wyschnegradsky, Rudolf Kolisch, and René Leibowitz. It was my good fortune, and that of many others, to benefit directly from their gifts.

Index

aesthetic judgments, 3, 4, 114, 160
aesthetics of music, 60, 159
alchemy in the arts, 126, 159
algorithm, xi, 43-48, 60, 62, 72, 159
alphaSyntauri, 76, 119, 169
Amiga, 98, 112, 118-120, 136
Anaximander, 87
An Electronic Studio Manual, xii
Apple IIe, 73, 76, 79, 120
Aristotle, 87
ArtMatic, 103, 104, 126, 141, 142, 159
Ashley, Mary, 28
audio compression, 59
auditory cortex, 32
Aurelio, 165
Austin, Larry, 28, 30

Berkeley Museum of Art, 79
Beyond the Event Horizon, 131, 140
Blau, Herbert, 24
Bliss Paint, 131, 136, 137, 140
Boulanger, Nadia, 167
Breeden, David, 169
Brün, Herbert, 72, 169
Buchla Associates, 31, 69, 116, 119, 169

Cage, John, 70, 72
California State University, 123, 169
California Institute of the Arts, 169
Caruso, Enrico, 166
Casio Digital Horn, 116
Celli, Joseph, 169
Chadabe, Joel, 28
Chaos Theory, 89, 141
Charles, Ray, 148
Clarinet and Friend, 93
common ground, xiii, 32, 33, 37, 38, 41, 53, 72, 83, 90, 97, 125
complexity theory, 4, 53, 159
compositional algorithms, 3, 6, 34, 45-49, 159
compositional field-tests, 19, 159

compression algorithms, 59-62
computer modeling, 62, 64
Corcoran, Ryan, 138
Crane, Robert, 168
creativity software, 159
Cunningham, Merce, 70
cyberspirits, 45-50, 158, 159
Cynthia's Dream, 109, 110, 122, 131, 133, 138

Dally, Lynn, 169
Darcy, Mary, 122, 136
de Oliveira, Jocy, 29, 169
DH-100, 116-118
difference in potential, 30, 87
Dijucontact, 136, 137
dynamical forms, 38, 160
dynamical systems, 37, 45, 71, 88, 103, 160
dynamic equilibrium, 95, 96, 160
dynamic graphic scores, 37, 39, 73, 75, 81, 93

Edwards, Carl, 51
Elizabeth, 131
emergent music, xi, 3-6, 34, 73, 107, 122, 126, 160
EMS of Amherst, 169
entrainment, 32, 35, 160
envelope, 35, 49, 51, 57, 118, 160
ephemeral forms, 4, 22, 27-31, 45, 91, 159, 160
Ephemeral Forms: Mother Musing's Flight Patterns, 22, 27-29
Euphonics International, 118, 169
event, 20, 23, 24, 28, 30, 41, 46, 58, 62, 76, 79, 80, 110, 125, 131, 140, 141, 160, 163
event horizon, 131, 140
evolutionary imperative, 3, 4, 38
experimental music, 72, 168
experimental social systems, 81

Fair Isaac Inc., 16
Fairlight Voicetracker, 98, 109, 160
Fanning, Cynthia, 109, 169
feedback, 4, 11, 19, 34, 45, 55, 74, 77, 104, 110, 113-115, 137, 138, 141, 159 , 160
FEELING AND FORM, 32, 77, 78
Feiler, Daniel, 131
Fisher, Margaret, 24, 169
flowcharts, 55, 57, 91, 103, 141, 159
Ford Foundation, 168
Fox, Deb, 125-127, 141, 142, 169
frequency, 30, 35, 38, 51, 52, 56, 60-62, 72, 88-98, 105-109, 116, 153, 155, 160-163

Frey, Kevin, 136
Fulkerson, James and Mary, 29

galvanometers, 93, 95, 96, 146, 147, 160, 169
generative systems, 12, 69, 159
generative software, 104
generic composition, 160
Gillerman, James, 169
Glasssongs, 76
Gleaves, Paul, 79, 120
graphic scores, 37, 39, 72-75, 81, 93, 160
Grateful Dead, 77, 78
Guy, William Allen, 155

Hafner, Everett, 169
Hanson, Howard, 168
harmonics, 52, 108
harmony, 22, 80, 88, 89, 112, 161, 165
heterodyne, 60
heterophony, 126, 160
Hewlett-Packard, 79, 80, 92, 112, 118-124, 132-135, 139
Hildreth, Valrie, 169
Houghton, Ralph, 166
Howard, Brice, 169
human feelings, 32, 37, 38, 77, 88, 117
Hunt, Jerry, 29, 169

IBM, 63-66
Illinois Wesleyan University, 110
interlacing, 95
Intermuse, 28
International Community for Auditory Display, 63
instantaneity, 29, 30
instrument design, 8, 50, 54, 116
Italy, 87, 89, 112, 165, 166

Jalbert, Greg, 131, 137
Jameson, David H., 63, 65, 66
Jenkens, Margaret, 169
Johnson, Will, 169
Johnston, Ben 29
Jones, Hilton, 29
Jones, Janine, 136

Khan, Hazrat Inayat, 49, 61
Kate, 146

Keb' Mo', 154
Keefe, Dennis, 74
Kenosha, 117, 166, 167
Kenosha Civic Band, 166
Kerr, Jean, 110, 169
Kitchell, Diane, 79, 132, 169
Kohl, Michael, 80
Kolisch, Rudolf, 5, 6, 168, 170
Korg, 118
Koykkar, Joseph, 169
KQED, 73, 113

Langer, Susanne K., 32, 77, 78, 88
laser animation, xiv, 37, 39-41, 56, 57, 72, 73, 75, 76, 79-81, 87, 90-98, 105, 106, 111, 112, 124, 132, 134, 139, 153, 160, 162
Laser Seraphim, 37, 40, 45
Lawrence Conservatory of Music, 167
Lawrence University, 87, 88, 167
Leading Edge Music Series, 109, 169
Leibowitz, René, 5, 6, 168, 170
Lewis, James, 29
Lia, 147
Light Fantastic, 119
Lightworks, 119
limen, 35, 62, 161
Limit, 88
Liquid Light, 113
Lissajous figures, xiii, 48, 91, 92, 161
Lissajous, Jules A., 91
London, Edwin, 29, 169
Luddites, 64

Ma, Yo-Yo, 149
Macintosh computer, 116, 119, 126, 137
Madole, Dena, 169
Malie, 153
Malinowski, Stephen, 74-78
Mann, Frankie, 169
Martirano, Salvatore, 8, 29, 169
Mary D. Bradford High School, 168
matrix, 4, 29, 30, 33, 51-58, 94, 161
matrix alignment, 4, 51-58, 161
McDonald, Lawrence, 169
media band, 11, 27, 111
Meg, 158
memory, 3, 32, 33, 37, 38, 51-54, 63, 74, 76-78, 83, 115, 165

Metaesthetics List, 51, 161
Metabiosis Series, 55
MetaSynth, 105, 108, 126
metatheory, 31, 161
MIDI, 70, 76, 98, 103, 109, 107, 110, 116, 119, 121, 137, 160, 169
Ming, James, 167
Mitka, Manny, 167
Mizelle, Dary John, 29
module, 22, 27, 39, 46, 48, 49, 55, 64, 75, 76, 114, 116, 126, 161
Montague, Stephen, 29
Moog, Robert, 20, 22, 31, 39, 49, 54, 64, 97, 116
Moog synthesizer, 20, 22, 39, 49, 64, 97
morphological resonances, 32, 77
morphology, 38, 41, 161
Moselle, Charles, 169
multidimensional matrix, 29, 30, 53, 54, 161
multimedia, xiii, 11, 14, 20, 21, 27, 37, 40, 45, 46, 49, 54, 65, 69, 73, 75, 97, 98, 110, 113, 115, 118, 119, 126, 161, 163
Multimedia Gulch, 73
Mumma, Gordon, 169
music synthesizer, 8, 39, 49, 55, 64, 75, 89, 91, 93, 105, 106, 109, 110, 161
mystic, 4, 34, 45, 48, 49, 87, 108, 161, 162, 170

NASA, 79
National Center for Experiments in Television, 73, 113, 168
National Endowment for the Arts, 169
National Endowment for the Humanities, 73, 87, 169
Nella, 156, 166
Nelson, Ted, 45
New Age, 123
Niblock, Phill, 169
Nicolai, Frank, 166
Nicolai, Pete, 117
Niehaus, AJ, 136
Nina's Song, 122
nonlinearity, 93, 106

Oberlin College, 20, 24, 72, 73, 87, 113, 168
Old First Church in San Francisco, 79
Oliveros, Pauline, 169
omnimedia, 21-24, 161
on-the-fly, xiii, 4, 19, 33, 47, 56, 75, 82, 87, 89, 110, 111, 125, 162
open art system, 22, 161
oscillographic images, xiii, 39, 48, 93, 161
oscilloscope, 22, 37, 39, 39, 48, 49, 64, 90, 93, 97, 105, 106, 161, 169
Other Minds, 125

Pacelli, Robert, 169
Partch, Harry, 8
pas de deux, 139
Peck, Art, 166
Penberthy, Debby, 122
perception, 12, 32, 33, 34, 34, 40, 41, 64, 70, 81, 88, 90, 158, 160-162
performance field tests, xiv, 161
performance-multimedia, 11, 21, 27, 37, 40, 45, 75, 97, 98, 110, 113, 115, 119, 126, 161
performance-videography, 110, 122, 131, 133, 136, 138, 140, 141, 162
periodic systems, 37, 162
persistence of vision, 95, 162
Petaluma, 39, 76, 79, 87, 92, 106, 107, 111, 118, 125, 145-148, 153-158
PHILOSOPHY IN A NEW KEY, 77
Phil's Float, 93
Piazzolla, Astor, 157
Pierce, Josh, 138
Pinzarrone, Joseph, 29, 31
Plato, 126
poetics of dynamics, 87, 162
Powers, Dan, 80
Premiere, 105
Pribram, Karl H., 51, 52
Project Artaud, 73, 168
protocompositional, xii, xiii, 89, 141, 162
psychophysics, xiii, 9, 11, 12, 22, 32, 33-36, 64, 65, 69, 87, 97, 161, 162
Pythagoras of Samos, 87, 162

quantum physics, 88

Raetze, Toby, 169
ragas and talas, 106, 162
Ravel, 5, 168
realtime composition, xii, xiii, 4, 5, 12, 19, 28, 30, 33, 70, 79, 80, 96, 103, 106, 109, 116, 125, 162
Realtime Electric Theater Band, 27
Rehfeldt, Phil, 93, 169
resonance, 12, 16, 29, 31, 32, 38, 42, 77, 88, 117, 162
resonant frequencies, 56, 92, 93, 96, 147
resultant tones, 56
Roarty, William, 169
Rockefeller Foundation, 73
Rosenboom, David, 29
Rosenquist, Willard, 169
Russell, John, 169

Sample Suite, 145
San Francisco Bay Area, 22, 27, 28, 73, 76, 79, 137, 163, 168

Santa Rosa, 79, 80, 92, 120
Schoenberg, Arnold, 5, 168
Schwartz, Elliott, 29
Scriabin, 170
Sekon, Josef, 29
Seiple, Bob, 52, 58, 108
significant forms, 5, 162
Skoug, Luke, 138
Slattery, Diana, 107
Smith, Jim, 80
SMPTE code, 110
Soft Candy, 111-113
sonification, 17, 63-66, 71, 97, 162
Sonoma Electro-Acoustic Music Society, 27
sound design, 8, 15
sound signatures, 41, 61
source tapes, 110, 140, 162
spectral component, 59, 82, 147, 162, 163
stereo sweet spot, 83, 146, 162
subliminal, 117
Super Gen, 118, 138
Synthi AKS, 80, 93, 94, 105, 106, 169
systems, xii, 3-5, 8, 12, 15, 23, 28, 30-32, 34, 37, 38, 43-57, 69-71, 76, 81-83, 88, 96-98, 103, 106, 111, 113-118, 123, 136, 137, 159, 160, 162, 169
systems analysis, 55
systems design, 49, 55

Taoist magic forms, 37, 40, 41, 162
Tektronix Inc., 169
Telecommunications Valley, 118
temporal lobe, 32, 41
Texas Instruments, 119, 169
Texas Tech University, 27, 52, 53, 109, 168, 169
Thales, 87
The American Federation of Musicians, 167
The Blackearth Percussion Group, 93
The Deb Fox Heterophonic Alchemical Tours, 125, 126
The Electronic Arts of Sound and Light, xi, xii, xiv, 21, 24, 27, 32, 47, 96, 97, 111, 119, 137, 161
The Exploratorium, 79, 163
THE LIVING ENERGY UNIVERSE, 115
THE MUSIC OF LIFE, 60
The Ohio State University, 72, 168
The Real* Electric Symphony, 4, 22, 27, 28, 79, 162, 170
The Tale of the Silver Saucer and the Transparent Apple, 49
The Unison, 105-108
time-based art, 32, 77

Tower, Joan, 169
transient, 60, 61, 163

U&I Software, 126
UC-Berkeley Lawrence Hall of Science, 79
University of Wisconsin—Madison, 5, 6, 14, 77, 87, 97, 122, 131, 136, 138, 168
Unlimited, 88
U.S. State Department, 170

variable, xiii, 4, 41, 43, 45-49, 62, 75, 79-82, 89, 91, 94-96, 109, 114, 116, 117, 126, 140, 141, 159-163
Victrola, 166
videographic fluid dynamics, 142
video synthesizer, 73, 79, 80, 97, 124, 131, 137, 139, 141
Vilas Fellowship, 168
virtual reality, xiii, 64, 163
visual cortex, 32
visualization, 17, 40, 63-65, 69-71, 105, 108, 169
visual music, xi-xiii, 3, 11, 22-24, 27, 34, 45, 57, 69-77, 80-83, 87-92, 95, 97, 105-110, 113, 114, 118, 119, 122, 125, 126, 136, 139, 163, 170
visual music flavors, 69
Visual Music Meditations, 45, 75, 90, 97, 98, 105-108

Walker, Donald, 29
wave characteristics, 29, 30, 162
waveform variables, 49, 160, 161, 163
Way, Brenda, 169
Webern, 5, 168
Wenger, Eric, 126, 141, 159
whole number ratios, 57, 58, 89, 90, 95, 96, 160, 162
Wilson, Olly, 169
Windswept, 116-120
Winter Reflections, 103
Woodbury, Arthur, 29
Wyschnegradsky, Ivan, 170

Ylem, 37, 79, 163

Zabukovic, Frank, 167

Printed in Great Britain
by Amazon.co.uk, Ltd.,
Marston Gate.